The Withholding Power

ALSO AVAILABLE FROM BLOOMSBURY

Philosophy for Non-Philosophers, Louis Althusser

How to be Marxist in Philosophy, Louis Althusser

Being and Event, Alain Badiou

Conditions, Alain Badiou

Infinite Thought, Alain Badiou

Logics of Worlds, Alain Badiou

Theoretical Writings, Alain Badiou

Theory of the Subject, Alain Badiou

Key Writings, Henri Bergson

Kafka, Howard Caygill

Alienation and Freedom, Frantz Fanon

Lines of Flight, Felix Guattari

Principles of Non-Philosophy, Francois Laruelle

From Communism to Capitalism, Michel Henry

Seeing the Invisible, Michel Henry

After Finitude, Quentin Meillassoux

Time for Revolution, Antonio Negri

The Five Senses, Michel Serres

Statues, Michel Serres

Rome, Michel Serres

Geometry, Michel Serres

Leibniz on God and Religion: A Reader, edited by Lloyd Strickland

The Withholding Power: An Essay on Political Theology

By Massimo Cacciari

Translated by Edi Pucci with Harry Marandi
Introduction by Howard Caygill

Bloomsbury Academic
An imprint of Bloomsbury Publishing Plc

B L O O M S B U R Y
LONDON • OXFORD • NEW YORK • NEW DELHI • SYDNEY

Bloomsbury Academic

An imprint of Bloomsbury Publishing Plc

50 Bedford Square	1385 Broadway
London	New York
WC1B 3DP	NY 10018
UK	USA

www.bloomsbury.com

**BLOOMSBURY and the Diana logo are trademarks of
Bloomsbury Publishing Plc**

First published in Italian as *il potere che frena*, © Massimo Cacciari,
Adelphi Edizioni, 2014
This edition published 2018

Copyright to this translation © Edi Pucci, 2018

Edi Pucci has asserted her right under the Copyright, Designs and Patents Act,
1988, to be identified as Translator of this work.

British Library Cataloguing-in-Publication Data
A catalogue record for this book is available from the British Library.

ISBN:	HB:	978-1-4725-8048-1
	PB:	978-1-3500-4644-3
	ePDF:	978-1-4725-8049-8
	ePub:	978-1-4725-8050-4

Library of Congress Cataloging-in-Publication Data
A catalog record for this book is available from the Library of Congress.

Typeset by RefineCatch Limited, Bungay, Suffolk
Printed and bound in Great Britain

BLOOMSBURY POLITICAL THEOLOGIES

Edited by Ward Blanton (University of Kent), Arthur Bradley (Lancaster University), Michael Dillon (Lancaster University) and Yvonne Sherwood (University of Kent)

This series explores the past, present and future of political theology. Taking its cue from the ground-breaking work of such figures as Derrida, Agamben, Badiou and Zizek, it seeks to provide a forum for new research on the theologico-political nexus including cutting edge monographs, edited collections and translations of classic works. By privileging creative, interdisciplinary and experimental work that resists easy categorization, this series not only re-assets the timeliness of political theology in our epoch but seeks to extend political theological reflection into new territory: law, economics, finance, technology, media, film and art.
In *Bloomsbury Political Theologies*, we seek to re-invent the ancient problem of political theology for the 21st century.

Contents

Contents

Introduction

Reprinted several times since its initial publication in January 2013, Massimo Cacciari's erudite philosophical meditation on the theme of the *katechon* in political theology might seem an unlikely bestseller. *The Withholding Power: An Essay on Political Theology* appeared as number 640 in the idiosyncratic but popular series of pocket-sized books *Piccola Biblioteca Adelphi* sandwiched between translations of Thomas Bernhard's *The Dying Goethe* (639) and Vasugupta's *Aphorisms of Shiva* (641). The *Piccola Biblioteca Adelphi* provided a ready audience for Cacciari's work, but its success also owed much to his personal reputation as a philosopher and public intellectual in Italy (see Alessandro Carrera's biographical introduction to Cacciari 2009). It also testified to the significance of political theology and its critique in contemporary Italian philosophy, politics and culture as well as the fascination with the Pauline concept of the *katechon* shared by recent Catholic ecclesiology and radical political theory.

The book represented an important development in Cacciari's already diverse, demanding but internally consistent philosophical authorship. His work as an author and editor from the late 1960s and early 1970s moved between political militancy – *The Capitalist Cycle and Workers Struggle: Montedison, Pirelli, Fiat* (1969), *After the Hot Autumn: Restructuration and Class Analysis* (1973) and the journals *Contropiano* and *Il Centauro* – to interests in the history and philosophy of architecture and German language philosophy, with Italian editions of Hartmann, Simmel, Fink and Lukàcs. In the course of the repression of the 1970s and 1980s – the Italian 'Years of Lead' – Cacciari joined other thinkers of the left including Mario Tronti and Antonio Negri in a fundamental rethinking of the logic of the political, in his case through the themes of crisis, rationalization and negative thought explored in *Krisis: Essay on the Crises of Negative Thinking from Nietzsche to Wittgenstein* (1976), *Negative Thought and Rationalisation* (1977) and *Dialectic and the Critique of Politics: Essay on Hegel* (1978). His inquiry took an increasing distance from dialectical logic and its cycles of staged opposition and reconciliation and opened itself to a thinking of crisis, decision and negation without any promise of a dialectical result or issue. It was an inquiry that traversed the work of Nietzsche, Weber, Benjamin, Schmitt and Wittgenstein, and would bring Cacciari's thinking into close but critical proximity with political theology.

In 1990 Cacciari published what he and many other readers regard as his most significant philosophical work – *Dell'Inizio* (*On Beginning*, revised and augmented 2001) – that challenged the basic assumptions of Schmittian political theology. A literally pivotal work, *Dell'Inizio* looks back critically to Cacciari's writings of the 1980s such as *Icon of the Law* (1984) and *The Necessary Angel* (1986) and forward to the geo-philosophical reflections on Europe *Geo-Philosophy of Europe* (1994) and *Archipelago* (1997) and the chrono-philosophy of *On the Last Thing* (2004), *Philosophical Labyrinths* (2014) and his most recent work on utopia with Paulo Prodi *Occidente senza utopia* (*The West without Utopia*). Strikingly *Dell'Inizio* closes with an extended mediation on the *katechon* that marks a departure in Cacciari's thought and a break with the dominant 'spiritual' tradition of political theology while also anticipating many of the themes of *The Withholding Power*.

Cacciari's work contributes to a well-established tradition of the critique of political theology in Italian thought and philosophy. In a memoir of the 1930s, the classical historian Arnaldo Momigliano commented on the discussions for and against Schmitt's political theology already taking place in Italy under Fascism. Schmitt's own tormented response in *Political Theology II: The Myth of the Closure of Political Theology* (1970) to Erik Peterson's 1935 'Monotheism as a Political Problem' (Peterson 2011) and its objections to the very possibility of political theology was in many ways part of an established German/Italian dialogue, with Peterson a long-term resident of Rome and opponent of any reconciliation between theology and the political. Yet the presence and power of the Catholic Church in Italian life ensured both the urgency of political theological debate and an understanding of political theology far more extensive and profound than its most recent expression in Carl Schmitt's eponymous 1922 article that first appeared in a

Festschrift for his teacher Max Weber. Taking distance from Schmitt's narrow definition of political theology as the inquiry into the secularization of theological concepts, Cacciari works with an historical spectrum that ranges across the Church Fathers, Dante, St Francis, Machiavelli, Marsilius of Padua to Nietzsche and Weber's theoretically sophisticated and historically rich accounts of the political implications of transcendent orientations for action.

The mobilization of philosophy in the struggle between Church and the modern Italian State in the 1923 'Gentile Reform' that among other measures made philosophy a prominent part of the secondary school curriculum ensured an informed but critical engagement between philosophy and political theology. This remains a striking feature of contemporary Italian philosophy, prominent in the work of Agamben, Esposito, Negri, Tronti and Vattimo. While Agamben and Vattimo seek in their different ways to find an accommodation between philosophy and political theology, the former in his *Homo Sacer* tetralogy and the latter in his work on *kenosis* and *pensiero debole* or weak thinking, Negri takes a more provocative approach in *The Labour of Job* by regarding 'The Biblical Text as A Parable of Human Labour' and with Hardt when appealing to a militant Franciscan ethic at the end of the first volume of *Empire*. The echoes of Pasolini's complex relationship with radical Catholicism are clearly discernible in the view of Christ and Francis as politico-theological militants. Esposito and Cacciari, however, remain the most implacable philosophical critics of political theology, with Esposito taking an even harder position than Cacciari in his

2013 *Two: The Machine of Political Theology and the Place of Thought*. In spite of their differences – exposed in a fascinating dialogue on political theology between Esposito and Cacciari (Cacciari and Esposito 2014) – both philosophers depart from Simone Weil's critique of political theology as the intrusion of Roman law into theological discourse and both suspect dialectical logic as somehow implicated in this intrusion.

While Italian philosophers are united in their *concern* with political theology the way they work through this concern differs widely in its emphasis and intensity. It is also undergoing constant revision not only in direct debates between philosophers such as those conducted by Cacciari with Tronti and Esposito but also in the broader development of each philosopher's own thinking. And no more so than in the development of Cacciari's thought where two distinct phases of the critique of political theology may be identified. The first, prevailing in his writings from the late 1970s and 1980s, returns to the sources of Schmitt's political theology in the *Religionssoziologie* of Max Weber and his distinction between this and other-worldly religious orientations. In this phase, Cacciari opposes mysticism and 'inner worldly asceticism' to 'political theology' as an essentially juridical discipline, finding support for his critique not only in Weber but also in the early Wittgenstein, Weil and Walter Benjamin. But with the publication of *Dell'Inizio* Cacciari inaugurated a very different, second phase of his critique, shifting attention from the radical philosophy of Spirit to the second member of the Trinity, the Son. It is the context of this shift that the concept of the *katechon* or withholding power rose to prominence and thereafter remained a keystone to his critique of political theology up to and including *The Withholding Power*.

Perhaps the most succinct and accessible statement of the first phase of Cacciari's critique of political theology is the 1981 article 'Law and Justice: On the Theological and Mystical Dimensions of the Modern Political' (Cacciari 2009, 172–196) published in the journal *Il Centauro*. In it Cacciari explores the parallels between theology/law and mysticism/justice through a reading of Schmitt radicalized by a return to Schmitt's Weberian origins tempered by a reading of Walter Benjamin and Simone Weil. Cacciari proposes to radicalize Schmitt's 'secularization of theology' argument by drawing attention to the 'intrinsic secularity' of the 'theological project'. Theology for him is intrinsically juridical, dedicated to the normalization of life through rationally pursuable ends. In terms that anticipate the later focus on the catechon, Cacciari gives theologically invested political form – political theology – the function of 'containing the secular, of comprehending its contradictions, so that its destiny may be fulfilled' (Cacciari 2009, 177). The juridical and normative containment of political theology contrasts with the 'ascetic competition' of individuals pursuing their own private mystical ends and vocations. Cacciari departs from Weber in refusing to harmonize what are for him the generically distinct projects of theology and mystically oriented 'inner-worldly asceticism' or the theological 'framework of the procedures and mechanisms that make up the modern state and its law (*jus*)' (Cacciari 2009, 177) with the mystical culture and subjectivations of capitalism Weber described in terms of the 'so-called

Protestant Ethic'. Instead, Cacciari emphasizes their irreconcilable conflict. The conflicts of mystically oriented individuals cannot be resolved juridically and they do not find in law a place where they can debate their differences or find an agreement. Instead Cacciari turns to Simone Weil's attack on theology's dependence upon Roman law and to Benjamin's notion of the messianic in order to align mysticism with a non-juridical view of justice. The mystical view of justice as an uncontainable break with the course of the world is irreconcilably opposed to any political theological attempt juridically to compose the differences between the transcendent and the mundane, with Cacciari insisting upon the 'antidialectical nature of mysticism' and its affinity to 'everything that exceeds the norm, the linearizing violence of the law' (Cacciari 2009, 185). He arrives in the closing pages of the essay at an opposition between political form and political decision, the former thought theologically the latter mystically. The derivation of the distinction between state and revolution from the opposition of political theology and mysticism is not intended to lead to their dialectical resolution but to the evacuation of each of the terms and their replacement by the technical management of political form without transcendent authority and through rationalized decision without political form.

By mapping the opposition of 'Law and Justice' first onto the distinction between law and mystical excess and then onto political theology and an anti-dialectical mysticism, the essay seemed nevertheless to engage its own dialectical movement of law and excess. It called on the law to *contain* excess and on the spirit of excess to *dissolve* law, effecting the paradoxical recapture of excess by the law and the ultimately complicit overthrow of the law by the excess of revolutionary decision. Cacciari's essay seemed to arrive at a revolutionary gnosticism whose paradoxes resembled those already diagnosed by Jacob Taubes, while remaining aware that this made its own oppositions very vulnerable to dialectical capture. After a further decade of work, Cacciari's *Dell'Inizio* emerged as the extended effort to lessen if not avoid entirely the risk of dialectical capture facing the opposition of political theology and mystical, gnostic revolution embodied in the oppositions of 'Law and Justice'. This entailed a break with the progressive philosophy of the ages of the Father, Son and spirit originating in the philosophy of history of the Calabrian Abbot and mystic Joachin di Fiore that would prove a powerful current in the radical philosophy of the twentieth century.

Dell'Inizio is Italian philosophy's *summa antidialectica*, a sustained effort to distance philosophy from dialectical patterns of thought. Its rigorously triadic organization indebted to Plotinus's *Enneads* comprises three books – 'The Critique of The Idea of Beginning', 'Mnemosyne, Time and Action' and 'The Epoch of the Son' – each divided into three sections that are in turn further divided into three sub-sections, challenging dialectical thought in terms of the very triadic structures to which it is indebted. In the first book Cacciari traces the triads of thought back to Platonic/neo-Platonic precedents and the Patristic mediation on the Christian trinity. The dialogues between 'A' and 'B' pursued through the three parts 'Logical

Beginning; 'The Crux of Philosophy' and 'Divine Trinity' of Book 1 range from Plato's *Parmenides* to Wittgenstein's *Tractatus* but are fundamentally structured according to the irreconcilable differences between Hegel and Schelling on the relation between the persons of the Trinity. Cacciari concludes after a sophisticated and detailed discussion of Hegel's *Phenomenology of Spirit* and *Science of Logic* that any focus on the internal necessity of the relation between the persons of the Trinity or on the figures of the Father and the Holy Spirit (as in 'Law and Justice') will issue in a dialectic inevitably biased towards the law and its reconciliation of differences. What has changed since his 1981 essay, however, is his reading of Schelling and the latter's focus on freedom within the Trinity along with the precedence of the Son. For Cacciari, emphasizing the person of the Son provides a way to avoid the dialectical capture inherent in the opposition of law and spirit. The revolutionary decision that he located in the spirit of mystical excess in the 1981 essay is now found in the paradoxical freedom of the Son to choose or avoid his 'fate' on the Cross and with this a rethinking of the Trinity from the standpoint of the Son and the radically undialectical character of his Gospel.

In the closing section of the first book there appear a number of intimations of the 'Age of the Son', no longer understood in the traditional or Joachimite trinitarian philosophy of history as a transitional point (the epoch of 'love') between the epochs of the Father's Law and a Future Epoch of the freedom of the Holy Spirit. In these intimations and more extensively in the Second Book of *Dell'Inizio* Cacciari distances himself from both a

political theology of the law and from gnostic revolutionary
excess of the spirit, calling instead on Schelling's anti-Hegelian
and anti-dialectical arguments for the freedom of the Son.
Revolutionary decision is no longer vested in the excess of spirit
but in the Freedom from beginnings of the Son. The focus on the
Son and his freedom would emancipate thought and action from
the inevitable dialectic provoked by the opposition between law
and spirit or the persons of the Father and the Holy Spirit. In the
concluding paragraph of the second section 'Divine Trinity',
Cacciari describes exactly what is at stake in his discussion,
outlining a philosophy of the Age of the Son that breaks with the
progressive philosophy of history culminating in the freedom of
the Holy Spirit proclaimed by Joachin da Fiore:

> The Age of the Son does not only signify the 'death of God' on
> the Cross that – on the basis of his spiritual presuppositions
> – Hegel can justifiably conceive as a dialectical moment. The
> Age of the Son does not just 'renew' that which it already
> knew: the inseparable relation between death and resurrection,
> between the hidden and the revealed, the hidden *and the*
> *coming.* The Son testifies to the radical mortality of intra-
> divine *life* by signifying his perfect distinction from any
> Beginning, and thus freedom. That this life continues to
> eksist, can continue to *re-veal itself* to be in the *whole* of its
> moments (concealing, withdrawal *and* giving and self-
> manifesting) depends on the freedom of the Son – but this
> freedom is not 'alone', does not speak in its own name but in
> the name of God in its entirety. Distinct from the pure

beginning, the life of God cannot co-incide with infinite compossibility – his life cannot not *decide for itself*. The decision of the Son is the perfect *icon* for the being intrinsically *decisive* that holds for all intra-divine life. *In* this drama – which can never exclude the possibility of a *no* – the Son decides for precisely *one* possibility: for the sake of life and resurrection. But at the same moment he says *yes* to *this* possibility, he hints at the other, insuperable and inescapable possibility that the entire intra-divine life sinks back into the *ek-* of his/its existing, in the Beginning that is this very *No*, in the very *No* that affirms the possibility that his/its being is radically mortal. God in his 'entirety' is truly at stake in the kenosis of the Son, just as the freedom of the Son – his freedom to *decide* for life – puts at stake the entire life of God.

(Cacciari 1990, 219)

The Second Book of *Dell'Inizio* shifts focus from the persons of the Trinity to the modality of their relation, trying to distinguish the 'other trinity' and the character of its internal relations from Augustine's view that relations within the Trinity are governed by necessity. The three sections dedicated to 'Chronos and Aion', 'Tradition and Revelation' and 'The Forms of Action' provide an important backdrop to some of the discussions in the Third Book of *Dell'Inizio* as well as *The Withholding Power*. The Third Book on the 'Epoch of the Son' and the later essay on political theology are indeed closely related. At the centre of the concluding book of *Dell'Inizio* – that is to say at the centre of its non-dialectical account of revolutionary decision and action – is to be found an extended discussion of the significance of the figure of the *katechon* that makes its enigmatic appearance in Paul's *Second Letter to the Thessalonians*. The containing or withholding power that in 'Law and Justice' remained firmly on the side of the Law of the Father is now located, problematically, in the Freedom of the Son.

The third and final book of *Dell'Inizio* is 'The Age of the Son' and is anything but a dialectical resolution or return of spirit to itself as in Hegel's Logic of the Notion. As with the preceding three volumes it comprises three parts – 'The Age of the World', 'The Name of the Son' and 'De Reditu' – culminating in a discourse on the *katechon*. The first part, as advertised in its title, reflects on Schelling's *Philosophy of Revelation* and the *Ages of World* and begins to describe the salient characteristics of the *Age of the Son*. The first of these is its radical difference with respect to the understandings of time and history informed by a philosophy of Spirit in the 'Age of the Son'; there is no dialectical movement of spirit recognizing itself in the recollection of the past and the anticipation of its future: the Age of the Son thus is explicitly distinguished from any Joachimite progression through the Ages of Father through Son to Spirit. The Age of the Son is one of a separation or *Scheidung* that nevertheless maintains the potential for a relation. It is a separation of Son from the Father and the Law, but also of the future as an *aion* from past and present.

The separation of the future from past and present defines the Age of the Son as one of freedom; in it the future as *aion* is wholly unavailable for knowledge or for any dialectical synthesis.

Cacciari draws on Schelling's *Ages of the World* to explain this unavailability of the future to knowledge:

> With respect to the Present, the Future is *always* future, and thus, if the Present is representation and comprehension of the world, the future will always be 'after the world' (*Nachweltlich*) which is to say it always remains further than any worldly comprehension. Every other 'future' is destined to end, to be 'reached' through the succession of presents – but the *Future* as an eschatological coming is aionically distinct from the Present. It is by force of this very distinction that the Present can conceive itself aionically, and not oscillate abstractly between being the effect of the Past and the cause of the Future. The *eschaton* will *never* be 'ready to hand' just as the past will not be 'known' or grasped conceptually nor the present nostalgically known or prophesied.
>
> (Cacciari 1990, 509)

Yet since the Age of the Son stands in relation to time as *aion*, it does not lack for false prophets who proclaim that the future has arrived and that the present is complete or at least is soon to be so (see Cacciari 1990, 615–616). And it is against these claims that the Age of the Son will direct its politics according to the katechontic strategy outlined by Saint Paul in the *Second Letter to the Thessalonians*. There are those who look back to the old Law overthrown by the advent of the Son – they are the impatient – and there are those who wish to calculate, predict or act in ways they think will hasten and guarantee the advent of the future. There are those unable to tolerate and sustain the paradoxes issuing from the Son's *command* to love or to recognize a life beyond law and the anti-law that it intimates – they are the dialecticians of spirit who do not recognize that the struggle between law and freedom is internal to the Son and not just between the law of the father and the excess of spirit. The opposition to the false prophets focuses on the *katechon* or withholding power understood as an anti-dialectical site. It is anti-dialectical because it contains or withholds both parties to the opposition, deferring any push towards dialectical resolution.

From this point Cacciari is able to describe the political importance of the *katechon*:

> The entire *political* dimension of the Age of the Son bears witness to such *aporias*: its principle is the same as that of the *katechon*. Every politics that would be *form* contains in itself 'sin' because, on the one hand, it does not will the failure of Revelation (that is in real contrast to perdition) but on the other has no faith in the apocalypse of the sons. It wants to *conserve* things, that is to retain *form*, for the *eschaton*; it cannot do so other than by withholding the rise of anomia – but it has no other means to withhold than to host it in itself, moulding it with its form.
>
> (Cacciari 1990, 631–632)

Cacciari frames the alternatives in terms of a Satanic politics of Behemoth or a katechontic politics that submits itself to the aporias of the *katechon*. In an intriguingly divergent reading from Schmitt he sees Hobbes proposing such an aporetic politics in *Leviathan*. Yet the *katechon* cannot withhold 'the war of each against all' for ever and to believe or even to hope so with Hobbes would be to succumb to another false prophesy. Cacciari insists repeatedly that the internal complex of opposites and civil war (*stasis*) that characterizes the Age of Son *is katechontic* and thus necessarily anti-dialectical and unavailable for any resolution or synthesis.

> The *katechon* works for its own end and for death in the most 'perfect' sense of the expression; every element that it 'convinces' to serve, brings it nearer to its end; every 'victory' defeats it, every form it manages to produce, dissolves it. Its containing-postponing-forming is a *drama* that cannot lead to any *catharsis* – a *drama cursed* by all its protagonists.
>
> (Cacciari 1990, 627)

Dell'Inizio thus ends with the *katechon* and its politics and ecclesiology of paradox and anti-dialectical movement. While it is anything but a redemptive politics, its commitment to striving to keep open the future does not definitively exclude the advent of such a politics. The political theology of the *katechon* knows patience and orientation towards an unknowable, unpredictable and essentially unavailable future. It is a theme taken up again in *The Withholding Power: An Essay on Political Theology*.

While *The Withholding Power* carries over much of the terminology and even some turns of argument from *Dell'Inizio* there are significant changes and additions along with an escalation of argumentative intensity. This is largely due to the occasion of Pope Benedict XVI's abdication and the relevance of the concept of the *katechon* for understanding Ratzinger's gesture of withdrawing from the temporal and spiritual power of the papal office. The event also provoked Agamben's reflection on the *katechon* in *Il mistero del male: Benedetto XVI e la fine dei tempi (The Mystery of Evil: Benedict XVI and the End Times)* that emphasized the younger Ratzinger's fascination with the fourth-century Donatist Ticonio's criticism of the Church as *katechontic*. There are a number of family resemblances between Agamben and Cacciari's books, beginning with their provision of appendices of original texts on the problem of the *katechon* intended to help readers understand the contested history of the concept. Cacciari's anthology ranges from Paul to Calvin but does not include the text central to Agamben's account of the *katechon* and extracted in his anthology, Ticonio's *Liber regularum*. Nor does Cacciari dwell as explicitly in his book on the specific event of Benedict XVI's withdrawal, while in contrast Agamben closely reads it in terms of Ratzinger's early work on the *katechon*, reprinting both his and his predecessor Celestin V's Declarations of withdrawal from the Office of Pope.

Both philosophers are fascinated by the implications of viewing the Church as a *katechon*, seeing it as both and at once the Church of Christ and the Anti-Christ, serving to hasten and delay the Second Coming of the Son. Both comment, Cacciari more extensively than Agamben, on Dostoyevsky's Grand Inquisitor, as the consummate figure of the Church as *katechon*. More fundamentally however, both philosophers work with the Weberian/Schmittian legacy of the conceptual opposition between legitimacy (or legitimate authority) and legality, finding in contemporary institutions of Church and State a growing indifference to questions of legality and legitimacy in favour of the technical. But while Agamben's text is strictly a *parerga* to the extended analyses of the *Homo Sacer* tetralogy, Cacciari's meditation registers an advance and deepening of his thinking of the *katechon* as a problem both for the philosophy of history and for conceiving the possibility of radical political action in the contemporary world.

The Withholding Power is divided into ten chapters that begin with an exegesis of Paul's second letter to the Thessalonians and its introduction of the figure – alternately person and thing – of the *katechon*. Each of the chapters poses and reflects on a specific question, departing from a reference to Schmitt's contribution to the revival of political theology and the question of the *katechon*. The early sections of the book address some of the answers given in the past to the question 'what or who is the *katechon*', ranging from the Church itself, to the Roman Empire, the Jews or the State. Schmitt's own implied candidate for the contemporary *katechon* – the Chinese Communist Party as a potential withholding power with respect to the global communism of the Soviet Union – is not mentioned by Cacciari although his book ends by reflecting on the contemporary global significance of the concept and its potential eclipse/realization.

The central sections of the book address the coincidence of opposites in the Church, sharing Agamben's fascination with the Church as *katechon*, at once the Church of Christ and the Anti-Christ. It analyses the problems of political form from the classical theory of empire to the modern state and returns repeatedly to the unresolvable tension between *potestas* and *auctoritas*. Obviously no dialectical resolution of this opposition is available, whether by means of the unfolding of spirit in history, secular power, class struggles or the fullness of time. Indeed Cacciari presents the coincidence of opposites as less a dialectical opportunity than a potential deadlock, reading Dostoyevsky's Grand Inquisitor as opponent and proponent of such stasis in all its senses.

While *Dell'Inizio* ends with the age of the Son and its difficult freedom born of decision, *The Withholding Power* terminates in the 'Age of Epimetheus'. The Age of the fraternal counter-figure to Prometheus (also central to Bernard Stiegler's *Technics and Time* project) is described by Cacciari as one of 'insecurity and perpetual crisis' with no decision on the horizon. This age seems to describe a *katechontic* waiting infinitely deferred and without an obvious *katechon*. Cacciari seems to suggest that the withdrawal of Prometheus in favour of Epimetheus marks the end of the *katechon* if not the *katechontic*, and with it the end of politics. The Age of Epimetheus is the age of technical rational problems calling for technical rational solutions – the eclipse of political authority – but the permanent crisis that accompanies this reduction of the political is not resolvable by a perpetual deferring of decision. This essay on political theology ends with the evacuation of both the political and theological and a vision of Globalization as Epimetheus roaming the globe discovering and releasing ever new evils upon humanity.

It is in the nature of Cacciari's inquiry to leave many questions open. In spite of some references to the Judaic tradition, is it the case that political theology must be conceived with Schmitt as exclusively a Christian problem or can it be extended to Islamic and other religious traditions? Cacciari's attention to Islamic philosophy in *Dell'Inizio* suggests that it might have a broader application, pointing to an inquiry that has perhaps become more urgent in the short time since the initial publication of *The Withholding Power*. The increasingly urgent references to globalization suggest that it is time to think beyond the Christian formulation of political theology. This is linked to the question of technology that already haunts the margins of the political theology of Weber and Schmitt and is addressed explicitly and with some urgency by Cacciari. But in both *Dell'Inizio* and *The Withholding Power* the response to the question of *techne* remains allusive and somewhat indirect, especially with respect to the relationship between the question of technology and the preoccupations of political theology. Finally the inquiry into the significance of chance in political theology – emphasized in the discussions of *tyche* in *Of Beginning* and Machiavelli's *fortuna* in *The Withholding Power* – opened by Cacciari needs to be developed further, especially given its destructive potential for any theologically invested political project. However, it should not be forgotten that *The Withholding Power* is an *essay* in political theology, that is to say written in a form – the essay – that was invented in an anti political-theological gesture by Montaigne and intended to raise and consider rather than resolve questions. And as the questions Cacciari addresses to political theology assume increasing urgency so too does the demand for more thought directed to the emerging form – no longer necessarily political but still trinitarian – of the relation between authority, emancipation and technology.

Works cited

Agamben, Giorgio (2013) *Il mistero de male: Benedetto XVI e la fine dei tempi*, edizioni laterza, Bari.

Cacciari, Massimo (1990) *Dell' Inizio*, Adelphi Edizioni, Milano.

Cacciari, Massimo (2009) *The Unpolitical: On the Radical Critique of Political Reason*, ed., Alessandro Carrera, tr., Massimo Verdicchio, Fordham University Press, New York.

Cacciari, Massimo (2013) *Il Potere che Frena: Saggio di Teologia Politica*, Adelphi Edizioni, Milano.

Cacciari, Massimo (2014) *Labirinto Filosofico*, Adelphi Edizioni, Milano.

Cacciari, Massimo and Esposito, Roberto (2014) 'Dialogo sulla teologia politica', *Micromega* 2/2014, 3–25.

Esposito, Roberto (2013) *Due: La macchina della teologia politica e il posto del pensiero*, Einaudi, Torino.

Peterson, Erik (2011) *Theological Tractates*, tr., Michael Hollerich, Stanford University Press, Stanford.

Schmitt, Carl (2007) *The Concept of the Political*, tr., George Schwab, The University of Chicago Press, Chicago.

Schmitt, Carl (2008) *Political Theology II: The Myth of the Closure of Any Political Theology*, Polity Press, Cambridge.

I

The Problem of Political Theology

We shall focus our attention on the problem posed by a single aspect of the relation between theology and politics in Western Christianity, one that has become central in contemporary debate thanks to Carl Schmitt.[1] It is the problem raised by the enigmatic words of the *Second Letter to Thessalonians 2:6-7*, which, even if not Paul's own, are certainly consistent with his doctrine. They speak of something or someone that/who contains–defers–withholds (*to katechon – ho katechon*) the final triumph of the Spirit of Iniquity, so holding off its own annihilation by the force of 'the breath issuing from the mouth of the Lord'. While the relation between theology and politics must always presents itself in historically determinate terms, it also poses questions of a more general theoretical order. Should we simply analyse the transformation of 'religious' ideas immanently

---

[1] For a broad analysis of the debate, see M. Nicoletti (1990) and more recently, G. Galli (2012).

according to the schema applied in the various enquiries into the process or destiny of secularization? Perhaps this assumes that the essential principles of Revelation or the Gospel – even before being 'captured' and conceived as dogmas – are able to be transposed or translated into constitutive elements of political action.[2] The expression 'political theology' cannot be limited to the influence of theological ideas on the forms of worldly sovereignty, for this assumes an original separation of the two dimensions; instead, it must comprehend the orientation or political finality immanent to religious life that underlies its theological elaboration. A relation, we shall see, that is neither linear nor completely resolvable, one that is in continuous conflict, and in which there can be no peace other than that of mediation and compromise.

Paul – or the faithful disciple who interprets or tries to explain his thought – returns in *The Second Letter to Thessalonians* to the eschatology of *The First Letter to Thessalonians* in order to warn that the Lord Jesus will not return until the work of his Adversary (*Antikeimenos*) is complete. His Day must be preceded by the full unfolding of *apostasy* (*discessio*), of the *mystery of anomia* (*mysterium iniquitatis*);[3] the mystery that is the epiphany of

---

[2] Such a perspective appears to be missing even in a work of such inflated proportions as Charles Taylor's *A Secular Age* (2007).

[3] A-*nomia* or active absenting of law is translated as *anomie* throughout. In Cacciari's own words: '*Anomie* means this: the Antichrist is in himself *anomos*, not because he represents anarchy but because he rejects biblical law. The *apoleia* (perdition) is connected to the rejection of the idea of Christ as the Redeemer. It is in this sense that the Antichrist is a destroyer, because he rejects the idea of redemption, he rejects the Gospel, i.e., the "good news", the "glad tidings" of Salvation' (Cacciari 2014, p.9) (tr. note).

Christ is followed by the apocalypse according to the force of Satan, of iniquity, of the one who *pretends* to be God and demands to be worshipped as God. The day of the Lord must be be *awaited* during the passage through this time of immense devastation. The end is *decided*. There is no *novitas*,[4] nothing *new* to discover. Nothing remains but to suffer with a martyr's resolve the ultimate assault of the ancient Dragon. It is the test imposed by the Lord prior to his victory.

Nevertheless another power seems to be at work in the spasm of this end-time (*eschaton*) one whose duration defies conjecture; it is a power that restrains the apocalypse or the perfect unfolding of the iniquity. When whoever embodies this power is removed leaving nothing to stand *between* the Adversary and the Lord Jesus, the latter will definitively condemn all those who did not believe in his truth. The Greek word for this power is first used in the neuter case *to katechon*, 'and now you know what withholdeth ...' ('et nunc *quid detineat* scitis ...') and then in the masculine case *ho katechon*, 'only he who now letteth ...' ('*qui* tenet nunc ...'). The present work will take issue with this *katechon* and its immense historical, political and theological significance. But first it is necessary to introduce the general context presupposed by this difficult biblical text and so permit the fundamental orientations of political philosophy associated with this apocalyptic vision of time to emerge.

---

[4] The Latin *novitas* (novelty, something new) is retained throughout. In the Christian tradition *novitas* means primarily radical novelty, newness of a radical kind; it also has the sense of a strange or obscure origin, the beginning of something singular and unique (tr. note).

It is well known that, with the exception of the *Johannine Letters*, the term *Antichrist* is absent from the New Testament. Yet the features given the Adversary in *The Second Letter to Thessalonians*, in the *Book of Revelation* and even earlier in *Mark 13:22* (the false Christs and false prophets who give signs and prodigies to beguile the elect) remain the same. This is the Hour – the Kingdom is now – but only for those who have *decided to believe*, who have *decided-to-be for the Event*. Such is the sense of apocalyptic time: in every instant every individual is called to decision; in every instant they are called to decide in the face of an *ultimate* either/or face to face with the *eschaton*: whether to live wholly in the truth of the Event or believe entirely in the 'energy of deception'. This call is addressed to everyone without distinction. The differences of traditions and customs, of class and language, in a word, of *ethos* are abolished. No longer *peoples* but *multitudes* of the chosen. The only thing that matters is the difference between those who live this time eschatologically and those who live it as a *moment* destined to pass over into other epochs, as a figure of history in which no decisions can ever appear final.

The believers now form the body of *cives futuri*, citizens of the future, prefiguring Paul's 'citizenship in the heavens', *politeuma en ouranois* (*Philippians 3:20*) in the steadfast hope of the true Peace of the heavenly Jerusalem. The others, the 'pagans', know neither the true city nor true citizenship – they are 'reactionaries' incapable of hearing the radical *novitas* of the Gospel, they resist only in order to survive. The *decision* separating those who hear and believe from the stubborn and the 'stiff-necked' is from the outset expressed in the image of two forms of citizenship: one that works here-and-now to *enfuture itself*[5] by understanding its present in terms of the promised future, and the other that clings to the present and works to insure and conserve its form. The first is the community of hope founded in faith while the second struggles for the *hopeless* end that there be no End! Although the conflict between the two is pre-judged, its torment and its history, as we shall see in Augustine, precedes our time and continues in it ever more intensively.

The *decision* for a future citizenship issuing from faith in the *novitas* of Jesus as the Christ cannot but express a permanent *eschatological reserve* against the exercise of any power whose main objective is to hold in form, to guard and preserve. In the eyes of the believer, the *auctoritas*[6] – the power that inaugurates, innovates, allows to grow and flourish – belongs essentially to whoever has raised the sword for eschatological time against every preceding 'state'. The Supreme Author is undoubtedly the Father but a Father who summons us to the heavenly *civitas* so freeing us from the father of the earthly city (*genitor*), from the generations and from the *violenta consuetudo* of the earthly city's ethos defined by Augustine in the *City of God*.[7] *Potestas*, worldly power, cannot pretend to authentic *auctoritas*. It may 'reign', in the 'secular' sense of the word *rex*, but it certainly can neither *lead* nor reign over final ends. Such prophecy makes it impossible for any State to 'be at peace'.

---

[5] *infuturarsi*, a Dantean coinage meaning to enfuture oneself. The term appears for the first time in *Paradiso*, Canto XVII, 98–99) (tr. note).

[6] *auctoritas* refers to an inaugurating and creative power. The *Auctor* is the creator God. In Christian theology *auctoritas* (inaugurating power) is authentic power and is often contrasted with *potestas* or worldly power (tr. note).

[7] *City of God, VIII, XI* (tr. note).

The value assumed by the category of decision, the idea of *novitas* opposed to all conservative power and the break of the link – ontological for Rome – between *potestas* and *auctoritas* are key elements of the Christian theological symbol *determining* the political dimension of the *Age*[8] it inaugurated. By representing these key elements, the *saeculum* in all its forms and conflicts finds its bearings in accordance with their meaning – a meaning that can only be understood in the light of the eschatological view of time informing those New Testament passages where the figure of the *katechon* appears. This brief time, the *spasm* of waiting demands interpretation. Is the *katechon* nothing more than an image of this deferral? Or is its power determinate, a *subject* consciously acting in order to defer the ultimate confrontation between the *incarnation* of Iniquity and the *parousia*, the full and perfect *presence*, of Logos-Truth? And what possible relationship could there be between such power and the *potestas* that merely 'rules' and shows itself in time *contra* the *auctoritas* of future citizenship?

Venturing an answer requires us to return to the general problem of political theology, for the essentiality or otherwise of the catechontic figure can only appear within its framework. The problem is to specify what form, riven by what aporias, political sovereignty can assume within the perspective of a theology for which authentic *auctoritas* is precisely what 'enfutures' us, a theology that seems destined to undo all will to form a 'state'. It is readily apparent that such theology cannot be favourably

---

[8] For translating *Evo* with *Age*, see Chapter III below and Cacciari's interview in Appendix 2 (tr. note).

disposed to any kind of power claiming self-sufficient authority. There can be no 'monotheistic' sovereignty. We may explain such reluctance in the light of the essential paradox of the Gospel, i.e., the paradox of *consubstantiality* within the distinction of Father-Author and Son, provided we know how to draw all the consequences from it, and provided we properly understand what makes the relationship between this theology and all forms of secular power at once highly problematic and unavoidable.

The tension of awaiting, of showing *forbearance* while waiting, renders any political 'confusion' between *potestas* and *auctoritas* intolerable and inevitably leads to understanding political sovereignty as necessary *in hoc saeculo*, in this time.[9] The time that remains cannot be 'disembodied' from the powers or the 'archons' who represent it. Those who have decided for the Hour at hand, the *believers*, must confront them – otherwise, on pain of sin, they will come to regard themselves as already immaculate, already spirit, already blessed citizens of the heavenly citizenship. Nevertheless, confrontation means mediation, and what does mediation entail if not compromise? Here we come upon an irreducible contradiction: to the degree that every power appears as a secularization of a theology which affirms the *sovereignty* of Logos it will be called upon to express itself as *mediation*. The *mediator* enjoys real command but *auctoritas* cannot be immediately exhausted in him, nor is he the autarchic source and site of it. Power *represents* – and for that reason depends for its authority on the *represented*, and while the believer sees in the

---

[9] *in hoc saeculo* (*en to aioni touto*), see for example *1 Cor 3:18*, is variously translated as 'in this time', 'in this age' and in the King James Version, 'in this world'.

nexus of Father and Logos distinct faces of the *Unum*, the One, in political representation this is necessarily impossible.

While the believer demands that power configures itself in the image of the theological nexus – and does not know it other than as power of *mediation* – his own theology reveals the radical inconsistency of this image. The believer reflects on political power from a theological perspective that views the sovereignty of Logos as *freely* expressing its full obedience to the Author and freely mediating the Author's will to the multitude, while at the same time recognizing that the secular relation between representing and represented bears no resemblance to the *exegesis* of the Father that is at work in the incarnation of the Logos. The relation between the 'faces' of God is neither adventitious nor contingent while in the political relation, in political mediation, no one properly holds *auctoritas* and neither can any *potestas* be from the outset 'believed' to be immanent to the Author who reveals and incarnates it.

For its own part, political sovereignty could not 'reign' if divested of every effective reference to the principle of authority. How can sovereignty reduce itself to mere 'representing' legitimated only by its capacity to mediate the interests that agitate and divide the multitude? For even the simplest representation implies interpretation. The act of representing cannot be reduced to execution – the act of interpreting itself already involves pointing in a direction, opening up a path ahead and the will to *lead* down that path. What authority can ground this demand? Only one that hails from 'above' with regard to the plane of mediation or of effectively pursued compromise. But *who* is 'above'? Is the one who holds power placed there by the represented in order to protect their lives? If so, the demands of the latter could always change – and the sovereign will always resist obeying them. The 'complicity' between the two dimensions is the realm of ontological *insecurity*. If the sovereign 'transcends' those represented simply by containing them insofar as his body appears to be 'composed' of them, then the sovereign's transcendence is pure artifice. What is more, an artifice that turns on the neutralization of that over which it 'pretends' to rule while the *auctoritas* of the theological symbol calls for a freedom capable of triumphantly *overcoming* its own *mere* humanity, one capable of *transhumanizing*.[10] Thus, the transcendence of political *auctoritas* threatens to make itself unrepresentable. Whoever projects onto this scene the theology of the Deus Trinitas is forced to halt before an unbridgeable abyss: in the theological symbol it is the same Author who presents *himself*, who makes himself present in the distinct face of the Logos-Mediator. And the representing-mediator is *en arché*, in the beginning and from the beginning, *one* with the Author. Here, on the other hand, the representation posits a substantial difference, in fact it is only conceivable by force of the difference between representing and represented in order that the two, always and at every instance, are also able to *represent themselves* as separate and autonomous.

For this reason a political theology conceived in the light of the *Deus Trinitas* appears even more problematic than one

---

[10] *Transumanarsi*: transhumanize, see Dante's *Paradiso*, Canto I, 70–71. Transhumanize means to go beyond the human towards God (tr. note).

informed by a pure monotheism. Yet it is only by virtue of secularization as its immanent possibility that we can understand the eschatological fullness of the idea of representation and the link between authority and power, of the relation in this time (*in hoc saeculo*) between the *civis futurus*, the future citizen, and every form of 'pagan' resistance. Can their compromise be founded on a merely administrative and distributive idea of power? Is the latter a force able to withhold *anomie*? In what way then would this force be related to the day of the Lord[11] and to the awaiting and forbearance of the *civis futurus*? In what sense may *anomie* be said to come from 'above'? Here the enigma of the *katechon* returns in all its urgency.

---

[11] In *1 Ts 5:2*, this day is described as the day of the return of Jesus, a day of rupture. In the *Book of Revelation* (*6:12 ff*) it is understood as the *Day of Wrath* (God's wrath against the unrighteous) (tr. note).

II

Empire and Katechon

We might ask: does not every constituted power that effectively rules perhaps belong to the dimension of the *katechon*? Must it not have at its disposal a certain catechontic energy? *Katechein*, more than the act of deferring or restraining, also means to contain or include within itself. Catechontic force has taken possession of the space that it now occupies and tenaciously holds it in its grasp preventing any of its elements from transgressing the limits (*lyra*), the borders of the city it has laid out (*de-liri*). The Hobbesian mortal god seems a precise image of this force, its true and proper *icon*, the creator of an exclusively worldly peace whose body contains all the *cives*. But can power subsist in a state of 'having been'? Can it be without its inherent energies continuously *de-forming* its figure? If it is a god, it would be life – but if its life is constituted by the multitude of living beings who are its citizens, it will depend on them. How to *contain* these two dimensions in one? The *katechon* must hold the multitude in its body, fistlike, while it must also wish to preserve their life. And life, such as it is, can never be thoroughly predicted, nor can its future be reduced to a mere *past*. It is even less possible that this god, who as mortal necessarily comes to be, must transform its own figure, alter its own 'constitution' and, in effect, call for its own *cives* not merely to respect the pre-established limits but also to follow him in going beyond them. In what sense then does the *katechon* restrain-withhold? Surely its political essence cannot be reduced to just this.

In whatever manner we choose to interpret the passage in *2 Ts 2:5-7*, which ever since Schmitt[1] has given rise to flights of biblical, juridical and politological erudition,[2] the political

---

[1] In one of his letters to Pierre Linn, quoted in the *Glossarium*, Schmitt traces the earliest elaboration of his theory of the *katechon* back to 1932. It is well known that this Christian Epimetheus developed this theory in his post-war writings as part of his enquiry into the problem of *ex captivitate salus* (*Freed from Captivity*), and in his 1950 masterpiece, *The Nomos of the Earth*. It may be that the footnote in the *Glossarium* refers to the studies on imperialism and the politics of power published by Schmitt on the eve of the victory of National Socialism in 1933. What is important here is the direct link with the theme of his work on Donoso Cortés and the political theology of Restoration (*Donoso Cortés Interpreted in a Paneuropean Perspective*, 1950). These works, besides Political Theology (1922), inevitably serve as points of reference in the present work. However, there is a radical distance between my and Schmitt's position both with regard to the analytical reconstruction of the problem of the *katechon* and to its philosophical and political interpretation.

[2] The term is not analysed properly in any of the important Lexicons of the New Testament (Kittel, etc.), nor in the various elaborations of the theme in political theology (there is no sign of it in J. B. Metz, an important figure in contemporary debates). The interest in the theme, even among historians of Christianity, stems essentially from Schmitt and the Schmitt–Peterson dispute. The most comprehensive reconstruction of the history of the term (*katechon*) is F. Grossheutschi (1996). M. Maraviglia (2006) relies heavily on it. These are texts dealing fundamentally with our specific theme, although references to the problem of the *katechon* can be found in many works dedicated to Schmitt in recent decades. For the place of the term *katechon* in ancient texts, one can consult the commentary of G.l. Potestà and M. Rizzi (2005). Some collections have recently gathered significant contributions

character of the *katechon*, the subject of this passage, remains quite problematic. The restraining function is undeniably prominent; Paul warned the community that the *parousia* of the Lord will follow the 'triumph' of apostasy and *anomie* and for such to be realized and arrive at its own apocalypse it must be preceded, in turn, by the liquidation of that which now holds it back (*to katechon*). The mystery of *anomie* in all its energy is already at work but it has yet to take out of the way whoever has the force of *katechein* (*ho katechon*). Both catechontic force and the force of *anomie* incarnate themselves; they assume the living reality of *persons* in a perfect inversion of Logos whose event *already* marks the Age, but whose *parousia* must *still* be awaited. It stands to reason that the time allotted to them, the *spasm* of time they occupy according to Pauline eschatology, comes from God – but how are we to understand the mandate of the *katechon*? Does it work from the *inside* of the Adversary's energy, signifying nothing more than what delays its full unfolding, nothing more than the simple fact that it is still becoming? Or does the *katechon* oppose it attempting in some way to prevent its apocalypse? Is it possible to glean this latter meaning from the verb *katechein*? With great difficulty, and in any case even simple restraining involves opposition, building a dam against that which would otherwise flood in. The main point is, does *political* energy

---

on the subject notably: *Katechonten. Den Untergang aufhalten*, in 'Tumult', 25, Berlin-Wien, 2001; *Il 'Katéchon'* (*2 Ts 2:6–7*) *e l'Anticristo*, M. Nicoletti (ed.), in 'Politica e Religione' Brescia, 2008–2009; *Il dio mortale. Teologie politiche tra antico e contemporaneo*, P. Bettiolo and G. Filoramo (eds), Brescia, 2002. On the *Antichristos-Antichristoi*, see R. Bultmann's very important work, *The Gospel of John: A Commentary* (1971).

primarily stand on the side of the power attempting to defer-arrest or does it stand on the side of the one who wants to rise, 'who opposeth and exalteth himself above all that is called God, or that is worshipped; so that he as God sitteth in the temple of God, shewing himself that he is God' (*2 Ts 2:4*)? Or again, are these two to be considered moments of the same process even though not necessarily 'allied'?

It is evident that the *katechon* belongs to a providential plan in which the entire time represented by Paul also belongs. Is not the 'energy of deception' (*2 Ts 2:11*)[3] also sent by God? The problem is whether the catechontic power can express anything *salvific* or at least beneficial, as B. Rigaux seems to think,[4] or whether it is merely the 'natural' index of a deferring of utter perdition (*apoleia*), or whether it is indeed an authentic *who*, a subject capable of resisting the presumptuous advance of the Adversary, or, finally, whether the nature of this resistance has a real political or spiritual, even spiritual-political character capable of truly countering the latter's power.

In so far as the first aspect is concerned, nothing in Paul allows us to view the *katechon* as a power working for our repentance (*metanoia*) in the brief time allowed to us. And in any case the community *knows* ('kai nyn. . . oidate') that it must be removed in order that *anomie* can triumph. Thus the *katechon* cannot be conceived otherwise than in the spirit of law (*nomos*). And what could in fact restrain, guard and conserve if not the law? Indeed,

---

[3] Cacciari uses the literal translation of ἐνέργειαν πλάνης (*energeian planēs*), *energia dell'inganno*. The KJV gives it as 'strong delusion' (tr. note).

[4] B. Rigaux (1959) pp. 274 ff.

it is not just a matter of simple deferral. What is at stake is a nomothetic will, the conscious obligation to pit *nomos* against *anomie*. Could this be the same as the *Nomos* of Israel? Would the energy of the *katechon* then be that of the people (*laos*) of Israel who opposed the imperial will that wanted to raise its own effigy in the Temple?[5] This explanation is plausible only from an exclusively historical perspective, possibly with reference to the time of Caligula, but it would entail having Paul consent to hastening the times, precisely what he seems to resist here, and would result in an outright or quasi assimilation of empire to the spirit of *anomie*. For these reasons, and for others yet to be considered, it seems impossible to abstract the *katechon* from explicit political meaning. Whoever defends or imposes the law cannot avoid political sovereignty, even if it is clearly distinct from any salvific implication. Pure *anomie* is indeed the 'reign' of the Adversary, Satan's incarnation, when his reign is finally established in its fullness.

Although matters may *seem* clear, further doubts arise. If the *katechon* is really opposed to the Iniquitous, why does Paul use an expression of impatience ('who now letteth *will let*'[6]) when referring to it rather than emphasize its anti-idolatrous value? Is it because such value is completely absent from the *katechon*? In that case, what form of political power is being referred to here, and does the *nomos* that it grounds exist in a separate or separable

---

[5] This is Santo Mazzarino's view. His important work, *L'Impero Romano* (2010) is fundamental to understanding the history of the relations between the Roman Empire and the development of Christian political theology.

[6] *King James Version, 2 Ts 2:7.*

dimension from *anomie*? (Here it would be necessary to insert the catechontic figure into the general framework of the Pauline conception of law.) And finally, does the realm of the Son of Perdition coincide with political anarchy or, even more, with the destruction of political form itself?[7] Let us begin with the question concerning the form of political power, since all or almost all the interpretations of the *katechon* have ended up identifying it with the form of *empire*.

In order to define itself as *imperial*, a form of power must be able to advance effectively the claim to constitute the destiny of an *epoch*. Epoch is a term that reverberates within the *katechon*. *Epoché* signifies arrest, an *insistence* on the same. *Epoch* is a lengthy period of time whose moments can be traced back to an essential unity, whose fundamental traits remain unaltered and whose events do not possess anything contingent but always refer back to the significance of the whole. The term *epoch* thus points to a time in which *history* seems nearly complete, in which becoming seems to bear the seal of being. This sense of the term epoch is here completely opposed to sceptical *epoché*. The latter implies a suspension, suspension in doubt until arriving, by methodical procedures, at rational evidence – it is a suspension of judgement during which a response can eventually emerge. *Epoch*, however, from the point of view of empire amounts to quite the opposite: every doubt and every crisis appears resolved in it. The *security* of the established order reigns. The term epoch,

---

[7] 'Son of Perdition' in the King James Version translates the Septuagint's υἱός τῆς ἀπωλείας, *huios tes apoleias* (Latin: *filius perditionis*). *Apoleia* means ruin, devastation and destruction (tr. note).

historico-politically speaking, designates the completion and the liquidation of every sceptical *epoché*. Within the epoch enquiry, *skepsis* must finally keep its *peace*. As soon as empire *speaks*, as soon as its *judgement* is pronounced, the *epoché* must fall silent; every 'suspension' is removed and *discourse* (*ratio* and *oratio*[8]) finally finds a solid ground on which to build its dwelling.

Empire always requires that thinking and acting turn into the deepening and further development of the given meaning of an epoch. A new epoch will not even be representable as such if elements of crisis and discontinuity persist within it. Consequently, there is an essential 'solidarity' between the idea of empire and a thinking that affirms as untranscendable the constituent factors of an epoch – admittedly factors that are put together in diverse ways but are nevertheless all pieces in a game which must in the end cancel each other out. Any form of critical thinking will cast doubt on whether the *epoch* is really *epoché*, on whether the conflict among its elements is merely functional for the life of the whole and can be resolved within it. To the idea of *epoch* as the supremacy of the whole over the parts and its corresponding idea of empire as the political form capable of leading all parts to the whole, 'ad totum ducere partes', there is opposed an idea of time marked by the ever open possibility of crisis, of decision and a leap.

If the great political form of empire as a *novus ordo*, new order, was born out of a formidable *de-cision* (tyrannicide is

---

[8] The word 'discourse' (Lt., *discours*) has a double meaning: reason (*ratio*), as in reflective intellectual and practical activity, and reason as oratory, public speech (*oratio*) in political deliberation. The term *logos* includes both meanings (tr. note).

often at the origin of empire formation), it can only last by means of *epoch-making* and a struggle to avoid further *de-cision*.[9] 'Messianic' time is incompatible with the idea of *imperium sine fine*, empire without end – and yet in a specific way it is an essential element of its origin. The contradiction is necessary, the same contradiction that time and again has been pointed out with respect to Schmitt: is his idea of political power *catechontic*? How are we then to understand the importance he places on the term *nehmen*[10] at the heart of *nomos*, on the gesture that first de-cides, then appropriates, and only after shares? While this tension *in abstracto* seems contradictory, it in fact expresses the very *reality* of empire: it cannot not 'withhold' inside its own epoch, it cannot not arrest-restrain the one who would want to 'judge' it, but at the same time it is always called to *pro-duce*, to lead *beyond*, to transform constantly its order and move beyond its boundaries.[11]

---

[9] The hyphenated 'de-cision' draws attention to the Latin *decido* from the verb *de-caedo*; the latter, when transitive, means, to decide, to cut off, to terminate, to hasten. The same root appears in the suffix of words for killing such as tyranni*cide*, regi*cide*, parri*cide*, etc., to which *de-cision* is closely related in this passage (tr. note).

[10] *Nehmen*, German 'to take'. The Greek word for law, *nomos*, comes from the verb νέμειν (*nemein*), whose phonetic proximity to the German 'nehmen' Schmitt is happy to exploit. *Nemein* means to 'divide', 'divide and share', 'deal out', 'manage', 'give one one's due' (the word *nemesis* comes from this last sense) (tr. note).

[11] Kojève reproaches the Schmittian *nomos* for privileging the distributive over the appropriative dimension of the concept. The criticism is pertinent only with respect to the concept of the *katechon*. The correspondence between Kojève and Schmitt (1955–1960), published in *Schmittiana* (edited by P. Tomissen (1998)), reveals a shared affinity on the fate of *depoliticization* (*Entpolitisierung*) but also a fundamental difference between their 'philosophies of history'. To the Hegelian prognosis, according to which history has come to an end, Schmitt opposes his own 'circle which has not yet been traversed' ('le circle n'est pas encore parcouru'). Yet there is no 'global

Catechontic energy is in itself essentially *executive-administrative*, producing security – but in the end it is a security impotent before advancing *anomie*. Empire, however, can be conceived only as energy that contains itself *in order to grow*, that arrests within itself any de-cision for the sake of the unrestrained expanding of its own dominion (p. 30). Empire cannot but demand *auctoritas*, from *augeo*,[12] its *civitas* is either *augescens*, expansive, or it is nothing. It contains the *katechon* but as a 'ministry' in the service of its own true mission: the universalizing of its dominion, of making the world its own 'system'. Here too the figure of the centaur asserts itself![13] For empire, epoch-making cannot be just the exercise of a restraining power since its own sense of power is pro-ductive. It is indeed within the 'body' of empire that the new must produce itself. It is the very *same* 'own body' of its sovereignty conserved through its own transformation. All *novitas* must already be *a priori* contained in it. In so far as the empire contains its own transformations, it *also* seems to be *catechontic* energy: a Proteus who is always equal to himself. Here then lies its essential difference from messianic time: the latter is properly *catastrophic*; it imposes a radical change of scene by virtue of the eruption of the transcendent on the horizon of history. Empire, though, renews *itself*, reproduces

---

planning' and even less a 'World State', the present moment should be seen as a transition to the friend–enemy confrontation among the *magni homines* (states as *superman*). For a better understanding of the background to Kojève's position his 1942 essay, *La notion de l'autorité*, is an invaluable source.

[12] *augeo*, Latin for 'augment', 'increase', 'expand', 'exalt' (tr. note).

[13] The figure of the centaur in Machiavelli's *The Prince* (pt. III) describes the double nature of the prince as man and beast (tr. note).

itself by renewal and the forms of this renewal have to be inscribed in the empire's *nomos* that is valid *erga omnes*.

According to this view, the political form of empire could never be confused with that of the *katechon* but, at the same time, one can also understand the reason many interpreters from the earliest times up to Cassiodorus, Jerome and beyond could see in the figure of the *katechon* the empire as such. The withholding energy that embraces and includes the drives of the multitude remains essential to the constitution of the empire that is at once conservative and productive. No law, no *positive* right could ever arrest its *libido dominandi*[14] – but this libido would turn into self-destructive anarchy were it not able to contain itself. The catechontic energy is directed as much outwardly to the 'public' as it is to the interior of power, to its *arcana*.

A 'deranged' empire becomes immediately an instrument of the Antichrist if not one of his *personae*, as in the case of Nero and the role his figure played in a number of apocalyptic narratives (*fabulae*). Not only is he represented as an intimation (*figura futuri*) of the Antichrist in the historic persecution to which Peter and Paul fell victim, but he is also pictured as returning at the end of time (*saeculum*) possessing the exact same attributes as before. Still, the tradition has struggled to identify him with the Adversary *tout court* for after all even Nero was an Emperor! For that reason Commodian's *Carmen apologeticum*[15] may be interesting. In that

---

[14] 'drive for power/mastery'. The term is first found in St Augustine's *City of God*, Book I, Preface. Augustine argues that the City of Man is dominated by its own lust for power and will be ultimately destroyed by it (tr. note).

[15] Commodian or Commodianus, Christian Latin poet (c. third or possibly fifth century A D) (tr. note).

recollection of witness accounts of the great persecutions the Christians suffered in the second half of the third century, the Neronian empire will be swept away, *removed* by the invasion of another king, a second and more powerful figure than the Antichrist, or the Antichrist himself as the head of four nations, 'who are not able to see suffering and pain' (*'qui nesciant ulli dolere'*), who are incapable of piety and who will burn the City to cinders leaving no vestige to remain. Then 'eternally shall lament the city that vaunteth itself eternal' ('Luget in aeternum quae se iactabat aeterna', 923). Nero leads Rome to ruin but the true ruin of Rome is the work of a 'second' Antichrist merely prefiguring the universal *apoleia* that he will accomplish in his own time, 'at the very end, when Rome burns, the time will be ripe' ('stat tempus in finem fumante Roma maturum', 925). It has always been very difficult to assimilate the *Roman* emperor with the consummate figure of *anomie* and *apoleia*, even Nero *redivivus*, reborn, appears in some sense as the *katechon* in comparison with the ultimate Adversary who triumphs over Rome.

Could there be a political form of the *katechon* itself? Perhaps *in abstracto* but it would not be imperial since it would lack *auctoritas*, and being devoid of *auctoritas*, how can it delude itself that it can contain, arrest and withhold *anomie*? And what if the *katechon* expressed its own specific political quality and wanted to behave like a force of pure conservation? A force of this kind, in the first place, would oppose not *anomie* but the empire itself. The catechontic dimension we previously considered functional for imperial power would *secede* from the latter and attempt to constitute itself autonomously. Its thinking would turn into a political and bureaucratic-administrative form founded solely on criteria of efficiency, on the economy of means and the rationality of ends. Such form will prominently manifest the renunciation of all epoch-making will. But how could a *katechon* as the expression of such renunciation *assert* itself in the face of the Adversary? The presence of a 'conservative' soul within the imperial system ends by undermining at its very root the capacity for resistance and by appearing 'complicit' with *anomie*. The more weakly catechontic and, consequently, more 'conservative' empire appears, the less it knows how to resist the assault of the Adversary.

Must we speak of empire containing the *katechon* as a moment and instrument when contemplating the *subject* who would mysteriously delay the coming of the Iniquitous? Only if we could radically contrast its *nomos* with the destructive *anomie* already at work ('energeitai'[16]). But now arrives the doubt, and not only for reasons emerging from scriptural context and Patristic teaching: can empire ever be peaceful? After all, does it not wage war against the saints? Is not its 'universal' worldly power represented by the fourth beast of Daniel's vision that devours, tramples and grinds everything down? Can the beast who comes up out of the earth, at the service of that other beast who first rose up out of the sea, to whom the ancient *Dragon* gave all his power and his own seat (*Book of Revelation, 13*), who is capable of seducing through great signs and wonders ('*semeia megala*') all that dwell on earth, ever be dissociated from the

---

[16] In *2 Ts 2:7*, 'energeitai', middle voice form of the verb ἐνεργέω (*energeo*), suggests that the movement of ecclesiastical apostasy was investing all its effort in *powering itself* towards a greater goal (tr. note).

figure of empire? Or can we pretend it is distinct from empire, like many Patristic analyses have done for tactical reasons, in order to avoid the open wrath of Rome?

Prior to being viewed in the light of these questions, the problem of the *katechon* must first be considered as an aspect of the more general problem of the meaning of law. No waiting for the *parousia* nor the imminence of the End could justify its elimination. Neither the divine Law-Word in its genuinely redemptive dimension – the one set down in the First Covenant for all time – nor the historical and political dimension from which it is impossible to be 'disembodied' could justify its elimination, indeed it would be a sin to wish it. But, as we saw, the empire's law cannot be interpreted as essentially catechontic. Nevertheless, can it still be justified? Can its claim to oppose the impetus of *anomie* be truly justified once we begin to investigate its internal aporias?

The empire that contains the *katechon* must by internal necessity be *epoch-making* and, at the same time, precisely because of this presence it can never really be successful in its task. The 'contingency' of catechontic action prevents it. On the other hand, should the *katechon* 'secede' from the unity of empire, nothing in the latter's power would be able to oppose the advance of the Iniquitous; and least of all could such advance be resisted in the form of an autonomously catechontic government, given that its energy would be spent, stifled between *anomie* and imperial domination. Such reverse is apparently the destiny of all purely conservative politics. But the law of empire is not 'holy law' where not a single iota is allowed to fall; it is only a law that 'guards' sin, 'provides it with safety' – and thus perpetuates it. In its autarchic immanence it cannot overtake the spirit of anarchy that erupts from 'below', out of the earth and the sea. Since the empire could not exist without wars and conflicts it finds itself related to the violence immanent to the spirit of anarchy. Catechontic energy seems to get out of the way by *itself*. Yet does not this statement directly imply an anarchic or nihilistic attitude in the face of political law? And is such an attitude compatible with the Pauline vision?

Furthermore, the figure of the katechon, once its political character is admitted, should be read in the light of the teaching of the *Letter to Romans 13*, where in full agreement with the biblical tradition, power, the exercise of sovereignty, its 'violence' seem legitimate because necessary. History is judged, the end-time has come but the *vulnus*, wound, of human nature is still open. However radical the relativization of every worldly power[17] may sound, however true it may be for the duration of this life, it is *commanded* by the image of the human condition tragically delineated in *Romans 7:14–25*. Even though I am no longer *slave*

---

[17] Paul's view of empire cannot simply be deemed nihilistic, i.e., an expression of a lack of interest regarding those forms of power that claim to last, to endure. The Marcionite reading of Pauline theology proposed by Taubes in *The Political Theology of Paul* is historically and philologically untenable (for more on this, see the recent commentaries on *Romans*, especially A. Pitta (2001), or the essay by G. Gaeta (2002). In my view, the most important essay on the subject is and remains M. Pesce (1986). The exchange between Taubes and Schmitt, from this point of view, paints the picture of an absolute divergence of opinion (see Jacob Taubes 2003). Taubes reduces the *katechon* to a mere sign of the adaptation of Christian experience to the world and its power. R. Panattoni (2001) has offered a lucid critique of Taubes where he, quite originally, reads the theme of the *katechon* as a time of stasis between *synagogue* and *ekklesia*. We shall return to this point.

to sin it does not mean I am *free* of it; I *now* know that the good does not dwell in me and at the height of my distress ('Oh wretched man that I am!'[18]) I know that to will the good is within my reach although 'I am unable to realize it'.[19] There is an abyss between willing and performing that only the Spirit that cries out, 'Abba, Father!' (*Romans 8:15*[20]), can overcome. The heir of God and heir through Christ is the one who is truly capable of this 'great cry' – but in waiting for the *apocalypse of the sons*, the powers that guard, punish and restrain are a necessary expression of *ira Dei*, the wrath of God. Not a gift *of* God but sent *from* God for our sinfulness. These powers are required by the bare *fact* of our *natura vulnerata*, wounded nature – whose meaning they 'comprehend' in all its senses, although they can neither prevent nor heal. In comprehending this wounded nature, they contain it *within itself*. They exist because sin exists and vice versa. They are suspended reciprocally in the spasm of time awaiting the Last Judgement. For this reason the discourse on the divine institution of civil authority in the *Letter to Romans* is confined within a majestic hymn to the *mandatum novum*, a new commandment summarizing all previous commandments: 'thou shall love thy neighbour as thyself'. Every law resolves and overcomes itself in this commandment; it is open to all and negates nothing. Any peace is only a temporary pact, an armistice before the 'overcoming of evil with good' (*Romans 12:21*). This however *frees* – frees from

---

[18] *Romans 7:24*.

[19] '. . . for to will [the good] is present with me; but *how* to perform that which is good I find not', *Romans 7:18* (tr. note).

[20] See also *Galatians 4:6–7* (tr. note).

the *duty* to hate the enemy, to vindicate the offence, to oppose evil
to evil, to bring to judgement. Nevertheless, even *in the end-time*,
which is still time, authorities, ministers and officials are required
by God ('per me reges regnant',[21] *Proverbs 8:15*), but they are like
the Kings of the First Covenant, a result of our sins (even the
greater and wiser among them were branded by sin).[22] Joined
in sin, empire and political sovereignty are separated from
redemption by an abyss. What epoch could they wish to institute,
being nothing but simple and fallen catechontic figures? All those
who promise eternity to empires lie; Virgil lies too (he at least lies
knowingly, for he puts the promise of eternity to Rome in the
mouth of Zeus[23]); what an immense lie it would be to affirm the
'reliability' of such figures! At the same time, we have already seen
that the 'person' of the *katechon per se* could not effectively limit
itself to the act of 'containing'. Only as will to imperial power, only
as consummate *libido dominandi,* could it give 'form' to the
rampant spirit of *anomie.* Put in these terms the action of the
katechon would necessarily end by exceeding the limits Paul
assigned to it, and if revealed as one that opposes *in principle* the
meaning which the Christian needs to give to the function of
exousiai – the political-civil worldly powers (*potestates*) – then an
irredeemable conflict would inevitably arise.

---

[21] 'By me Princes rule, and Nobles, even all the Judges of the earth', *KJV, Proverbs 8:15*
(tr. note).

[22] Therefore, it is not enough to state, with Schmitt (2015, 32–33) that 'only the *will* to
power is evil', but power 'remains in its essence good and divine'. It is in fact an *evil*
spirit of God that takes possession of Saul (*1 Samuel 16:14*)!

[23] Augustine, *Sermon 105*; Virgil, *Aeneid* 1: 278–288 (tr. note).

III

Epoch and Age

Can imperial power be reduced to a catechontic dimension without forfeiting its epoch-making will? Is it possible to relativize and contain imperial power within the ambit of 'render unto Caesar' (we shall soon come to understand the importance of this saying) without exhausting its energy? And, finally, should these questions be answered affirmatively, will it be possible to establish a substantial link between the political and eschatological dimensions? Already these questions assume we are armed with the patience of waiting, for if we were to know that the Day of the Lord is *now*, it would make no sense to obey any worldly power. At the same time, no 'mortal God',[1] no power concealing the fact that *this* is the end of time can be tolerated. In this *time* the exercise of political power is necessary and its authority therefore is providential, but providential only insofar as it is *for its own death*. Power must be *effective* – it cannot reduce itself to functions

---

[1] The thinly veiled debate with Hobbes' Leviathan is pursued through these early chapters; Cacciari has in mind the frontispiece to *Leviathan* with its sovereign body politic made up of the bodies of the individual citizens.

of administration or 'policing' – and in order to be effective it cannot but will to be 'epoch-making'. However, the epoch it marks is just as much the epoch of its own death. Only this self-consciousness allows power to assume an eschatological character. Let us try to understand how we can undo these seemingly inextricably knotted lines of enquiry.

The universalistic vocation of imperial power understood as 'iconic' sovereignty demands that time be understood in the light of values, contents and forms of life that *endure*. Were the unity of the epoch to break down, the spatial integrity of empire would also be torn apart. The crisis of the times is accompanied by the splitting and opposing of places. Different temporalities belong to different spaces and vice versa. This occurred in the dissolution of the *respublica christiana*, between the twelfth and thirteenth centuries with the irreconciliability of the 'times' of communal freedom, of new state formations and old feudal orders with the continued reign of the idea of Empire (*Sacro Romano Imperium*). The empire's capacity for 'epoch-making' was not recognized by any of these diverse powers. They were only prepared to recognize its weak *catechontic* authority as, in the last instance, a source of security and guarantor of autonomously agreed pacts (an idea that completely opposes that of the twelfth-century Hohenstaufen Chancellery and its pronouncements on the *Sacrum Imperium*). The idea of sacredness (of the King as 'God's Anointed' on a par with the Priest) continued to hold sway but only to the extent it could delay the collapse of the empire.[2] The new powers would

---

[2] See Herfried Münkler (2007).

never have accepted that there was no salvation (*nulla salus*) outside the unity of the empire.[3] From this point of view, modern thought – heir and 'accessory' to those powers – has battled against the very idea of empire, considering it to be nothing more than an abstract system devoid of the force that constitutes the essence of a State. A victorious battle – at least up to now.[4]

Must not those who understand political power in the light of Pauline eschatology hold a similar position? They can recognize the legitimacy of the epoch-making requirement of political power, but only if it may be recollected in the light of the Age. Every worldly power and its laws wants and needs to *endure* and in some way suspend the flux of life's forms. Paradoxically this enduring has to be reduced to an *instant*. And all *instants* are subsumed in the Now of the last Age, the end-time forever marked by the apocalypse of the Logos. *Age* is *Aion*, eternity, eternal Life, revelation of eternity in time – as well as the place where such revelation re-presents itself as necessarily superior to all the places where one tirelessly strives to contain the chaotic energies of becoming. Here the difference of principle collapses: while the authority representing the ultimate meaning of the Age re-*presents* it in itself (or rather, it is *analogous* to that meaning which '*makes itself present*' in it)[5] in the cult

---

[3] Cacciari here applies the maxim *extra ecclesiam nulla salus* – there is no salvation outside of the church – to the claim of empire to be the only power capable of providing security, a claim contested by the new powers (tr. note).

[4] On liberal thought's criticism of the idea of empire (following the development of Hegelian political philosophy from the young Hegel's *The German Constitution* up to the *Lectures on the Philosophy of History*) see P. Catalano (1986 and 2000).

[5] On the theological and political problem of 'representation' see Hasso Hofmann (2007); Giuseppe Duso (2003) follows Hofmann.

that it regulates above all and whose monopoly it enjoys, the worldly *exousia*[6] sets about constructing for itself the idea of epoch and representing it. Epoch is a representation of *exousia* and is in a certain sense its first and essential *production*, its *Weltanschauung*.

According to the 'measure' of the Age, however, the epoch can be no other than its image always on the verge of turning into a mere *eidolon* (idol) to which no self-sufficiency can be attributed. Our destiny, our destination is only legible prophetically and eschatologically in the signs of the Age. In other words, the epoch expresses nothing but *values*, that is evaluations, points of view, ideologies while the eternal reveals itself in the Age. Every epoch is in this way 'pre-judged' in the Age that encompasses and 'surpasses' it. By analogy the same relation should subsist among the powers that embody the two concepts of time. The epoch-making power should never claim to represent the Age because *de facto* it is not so, as one can see in the rise and fall of empires already prophesied in the *Book of Daniel*,[7] but also because *de jure* the Age reveals itself and cannot be represented by any means other than itself. While it is proper that empire closely approximates the true image of the Age, it must also convince itself of the superiority of the meta-political *auctoritas* of the

---

[6] *exousia*: authorized, delegated power or authority; rule. In Pauline theology (esp. in *1 Corinthians*), *exousia* comes to mean power to decide (for oneself), and hence free will, freedom or liberty (tr. note).

[7] On the significance of the succession of empires in Daniel's prophesy, see A. Momigliano (1987); in the same volume, see also *Il cristianesimo e il declino dell'impero*. The latter has made an immense contribution to the present work.

hora novissima[8] (neither anti- nor a-political), which sets itself to work as memory and care through all the epochs and their empires that will conclude the sorrowful odyssey.

Between epoch and Age there is both connection and conflict, *polemos*. Whoever represents the epoch must 'pass' it off as the Age, pretend that it is the Age while those who firmly *believe* themselves to be its authentic manifestation on earth always tend either to deny any truth to the values of the epoch or to subject them to their own authority and order them accordingly. The most widely diverging ways of compromise just as much as the most brutal conflicts are possible in this *polemos* while synthesis can only be apparent or coincide with the collapse of all significance attached to the Age; when the experience of time contracts to that of the epoch and its 'world views' then all enquiry into the *eschaton* ceases to preoccupy us. The end of the conflict will be none other than the decline of those who in this conflict stood as a sign of contradiction and whose very existence claimed an *eschatological reserve* with respect to all the powers of the epoch.

Nevertheless, the tie that binds epoch and Age seems to rule out the survival of only one of the duellists. This fact is reflected in the realism of the Pauline conception of worldly power. If empire does not aim to make itself something *more* than epoch then it will also cease to function effectively as *defensor pacis*,

---

[8] *novissima* literally means 'the newest'. It paradoxically translates the Greek 'eschaton', meaning 'the very last'. In Christian theology 'the very last' is simultaneously 'the very first', thus *Hora novissima* is usually rendered as '*the Last Hour*' that is also the very First Hour (tr. note).

defender of the peace – if spiritual power *now* believes itself free
from all worldly authority then it commits the sin of impatience
by claiming to bring forward the Last Judgement. The end of the
conflict through the collapse of one of the parties only proves the
impotence of the victor – one of the most profound and least
understood themes of Hegel's philosophy of history. Thus in the
destiny of Europe the decline of the 'guardian' of the Age was
accompanied by that of an epoch-making (*epoche-machende*)
imperial power. The collapse of the idea of Age took with it the
idea of a form of power genuinely capable of *enduring*. 'Where
are the princes of the heathen? ... They vanished and are gone
down to the grave' (*Baruch 3:16–19*).

The Church never challenged the Empire from the point of
view of the new state-powers, mainly because the *love* which
inspired and drove them would not submit itself to the Age. The
episkopos[9] (overseer) 'of those who stand outside' had to limit
himself to the role of sovereign, but in the narrow sense of
'disciplining and punishing' and attending to *necessitates saeculi*,
to worldly needs. Paradoxically, for the empire to arrange itself in
like manner would have required it to intervene in dogmatic
controversies (as was the case with Constantine) to the point of
openly competing with the authority of the Church. If the empire
took its bearings from the sun of the Age it would not have
tolerated a merely catechontic self-representation. However, in

---

[9] *episkopos*, ἐπίσκοπος, literally means 'overseer', he who is charged with the task of
'keeping an eye on Christ's flock'. In the NT also designates one of the positions of
leadership in the Church (tr. note).

seeking to be 'sacred' it sustained an unbreakable bond of friendship/enmity with the Church. Catastrophe struck with the appearance of a power that not only defined itself as in principle autonomous from every spiritual power but also as one that could not even tolerate any such above itself, even more: one that was incapable of understanding or heeding spiritual claims. Paradoxically the Church always sought a catechontic power invested with spiritual authority like steel wood or a heroic centaur.[10] With the collapse of this idea nothing remains but the mortal and de-sacralized form of the State. The epoch of empire declines into a *techne politiké* (political technique) of endurance that pours the eschatological question out into the infinite void of becoming. A State can only *fake* epoch-making, just as a nationalistic *Reich* faked being an empire. But empire can only be conceived in its *difference* (opposed to *in-difference!*) with the eschatological order for which spiritual authority is a living memory. The latter becomes mere *preaching* when confronted with indifferent catechontic powers that are no longer empires and that fight among themselves in their ever more desperate quest to bestow the sign of the Age on their own particular epoch.

---

[10] 'un legno d'acciaio', lit. 'steel wood', refers to the Church's impossible synthesis of eschatology and political *praxis*; they can neither be reconciled nor separated. 'Heroic centaur' suggests Machiavelli and perhaps refers to the same impossible synthesis viewed from the standpoint of Empire or Prince (tr. note).

IV

Quis est Katechon?

Our received ideas of power, sovereignty and the relationship between political and religious, worldly and spiritual authority continue to be informed, even though we are hardly aware of it, by a jumble of theological-political issues stemming from the set of relations just described. They are questions that 'secularization' as the dissolution of every idea of epoch conceals in itself rather than resolves or overcomes.

We have already encountered the fundamental contradiction undermining the figure of the *katechon*: if it is to *matter* (*se essa deve valere*) it will inevitably have to turn or try to turn itself into empire, but the latter will necessarily compete with other authorities to represent the Age. How can its *potestas* otherwise restrain, contain and withhold *anomie*? At the same time, is not the claim to represent the ultimate meaning of the Age within epochal time not the very sign of *anomie*? For its part, when the Church claims to know and expectantly await the End with certain hope it affirms that it is the 'place' where the Age represents itself while never accepting a similar claim by another power.

When it comes to the *eschaton* every empire must leave the last
word to the pilgrim, to the *civis futurus*, to the community that
on earth stands for the true image of *politeia en ouranois*, of
celestial citizenship. This is the only holy city, the only good
promised by the Lord, and all hope whose seed is preserved in
the heart of the believer turns towards it (Augustine, *Psalm 105*).

But how could the *civis futuris* not claim to speak on all aspects
of civil life, especially when the ultimate meaning of shared history
can only become fully comprehensible in the light of the *eschaton*.
This is an open and irrepressible asymmetry that is intolerable for
imperial power. And why not for a merely catechontic power? It
may become able blandly to 'put up with' the sermons of spiritual
authority but only at the cost of powerlessness, even to feign some
auctoritas and thus showing itself every day to be incapable of
fulfilling its *officium*, its mission, to serve as a barrier against *anomie*.

How is opposition to the advance of *anomie* conceivable in
an apocalyptic context if we remain indifferent to the meaning
of the *eschaton*? Such opposition would have only the stamp of
an autarchic will to endure, a will to survive but not oppose
the Adversary; perhaps it is even a sign of covert complicity
with him? But if as seems to be the case the *katechon* wants to
become epoch-making in thus assuming some kind of imperial
physiognomy, it must withhold, arrest and *contain* above all
whoever disputes or denies the *autonomy* or power to constitute
law by its own means characteristic of empire. This entails
opposition to the eschatological community. How will the
katechon be able to do its work in a productive-constructive way
if it finds itself, in at least in one of its guises at the service of the

Adversary, of the spirit of *apoleia*, of destruction? Whether catechontic power is forced into an exclusively functional/ instrumental role or whether it assumes imperial form, it seems to risk itself at the borders or even inside the realm of *timê*,[1] of the Iniquitous. If this is the outcome then the *anomie* of the latter can no longer simply appear as the absence of *nomos*. The ultimate power advancing before the Last Judgement is such in every sense. It is there in the commander, it is hierarchy, organization and worship. The final catastrophe does not announce itself with anarchic *chaos* nor in the savage features of the Forester in Ernst Jünger's *On the Marble Cliffs*, but through the metamorphosis of imperial form into the figure of an *unheard-of (in-audito)* empire that 'overcomes' both the figure of the *katechon* and that of earthly *auctoritas* while wrestling with the Church for spiritual supremacy.

Before addressing the last question, we need to take a closer look at the catechontic traits that can be 'detained' by empire and then enquire into the relation or compromise that spiritual authority might attempt to establish with them.

Quid o quis est katechon, who or what is the katechon? The context of Paul's preaching (both in the pseudepigraph *2 Ts* and in *1 Ts*) is the eschatology of *Matthew 23–24* (and its parallels in the Gospels of *Mark* and *Luke*), of the *First Letter of John*, of the *Book of Revelation* and in the most ancient Christian literature of

---

[1] τιμή (*timê*): honour, honour by reason of rank or office, received and perceived honour; reverence; price, value. *Timê may* refer here to the culture of honours paid to heroes and gods in cult. In short, it is another word for ritual. When faith is absent, worship is no longer reverence but mere ritual, i.e., *timê* (tr. note).

the *Didache, 16:1–7*. The Adversary who presents himself as God demands to be worshipped as the One God, and to fight with God on the same ground of the most rigorous monotheism ('he will topple the idols in order to make them believe that he is God', Irenaeus, *Adversus Haereses*, V, 25.1; incidentally, Irenaeus is the first to cite the *Second Letter to Thessalonians*). This Adversary cannot be confused with any form of 'reactionary', polytheistic or pagan nostalgia and will only be defeated by the breath of the Lord, by Spirit. Therefore the energy of the Adversary is much more potent than any catechontic force and will only surrender to the *parousia* of the *Kyrios*, the Lord Jesus.

But first, it is essential to understand properly the novelty represented by the figure of the Son of Perdition for it fully participates in the *novitas* of the Logos incarnate and the Age it inaugurates. The Deceiver of the world presents himself as the Son of God (*Didache, 16:4*), and his energy is expressed in *seducing* from faith in the Lord Jesus: his apostasy is not a vague *discessio* or *secession* from God and has nothing to do with any form of 'atheism'; it has only one target – to eradicate faith in Jesus as the Christ. The Son of Perdition is the Antichrist, and as such only conceivable within this Christian Age. It is not possible to oppose Christ, to be *Antikeimenos*[2] through the power of the ancient idols. To *a* Son there must be opposed *the* Son: to a spirit of *apoleia* (destruction) that of *soteria* (salvation). Whatever

---

[2] *Antikeimenos* (the Adversary), from the verb *antikeimai* (to confront, to oppose), literally means 'he who opposes, who is against (*anti*)' (tr. note).

opposes this apocalyptic *duellum* will be crushed and all that is 'lukewarm' will be spat out. Everything stands helpless before the power of the *Antikeimenos* whose own impotence before the Lord will reveal itself only at the very last.

Thus without doubt the *katechon* will be swept away, but will it be swept away by the One Idol[3] who is 'anti-idolatrous' with respect to every previous form of idolatry because he really experiences these as an effective obstacle? Or will it be swept away by the *prayers* of those who with steadfast hope yearn for the Lord's breath (*pneuma*)? In the first case one could think of a 'compromise' between those waiting in faithful forbearance and the *katechon*; in the second case, of a 'perspective' shared by the Christian and the *Antikeimenos* since both long to hasten the elimination of the withholding power. The verdict on the nature of the katechon will change radically according to the response it provokes.

It is clear that the power of the *katechon* is inscribed *a priori* in the abyss of the divine will. The same holds for the force of Satan sent by God to condemn those who do not welcome the love of truth (*agape tes aletheias*). Neither *katechon* nor Adversary have the effective power to delay or hasten the *parousia*. The Last Day comes like a thief in the night and not even the Son knows the hour (*Matthew 24:36, 43; 1 Ts 5:2; Rev 16:15*). It is written that *before* that day the full uncovering of the apostasy must first

---

[3] 'Idolo Uno'. A reference to *Irinaeus of Lyon, Against Heresies, Book V, XXV, 1*, who speaks of the *Antikeimenos* as the one who strives to become the *One Idol* after taking all other idols out of the way and installing himself as God in the place of the true God (tr. note).

be completed. The drama is real for precisely this reason. The brief time, the pre-judged time stretching before us has not yet acquired the shape that it will come to assume. It is a stage for proto-agonists and not for puppets. These carry out their 'missions' without being able to know where it will end. What is clear and inalterable is the mere meaning of these 'missions'. History is their manifestation and confirmation – but it is nevertheless history, an authentic *agon*, a conflict between the wills to power of real subjects. And thus even catechontic force is a containing-withholding *subjectivity* just as vital as that of the *Antikeimenos*, who only exists in the life of those who act as *antichrists* according to the words of the *First Letter of John, 2:18–23*, whose dramatic force far exceeds that of the Pauline *Antikeimenos* (and even more noticeably that of the *antikeimenoi* of the *First Letter to Corinthians 16:9*, where the term is reserved for those who oppose the Apostle of the Gentiles). The Antichrist forms a *community* in the inverted image of the *ekklesia*. It has a *body* made up of those who, having fallen for the deception, act as antichrists. In the Hour at hand the energy of this community becomes uncontainable. As proof of its full belonging to the Age, it is constituted by many who 'came from us' (*1 John, 19*), even if by their nature they were not 'of us'. These words can only be understood this way: the Antichrist shows all his power in dividing (*diabolos*) the Church, wrenching from its midst all those who do not belong there in *gratia*. In his *Treatise on John's Epistle* Augustine went further and forcefully argued that many antichrists revealed themselves and left our Church, but there are many who still remain (*'multis intus sunt, no exierunt, sed tamen antichristi sunt'*), and everyone must ask themselves whether they too are not one of their number.

Might not 'those who remain' be numbered among the ranks of the catechontic powers? The *katechon*, in fact, must be understood as plural as we have done up to now, but not just as a civil and political plurality. The antichrists who remain in the Church impartially exercise the function of containing and restraining; they hold back the day when the ranks of the Antichrist will be completely filled and the last battle must take place. Why, indeed, would they not make their 'exit', if they did not will to defer the *pleroma* of the power of the Iniquitous? Is there then a possible *catechontic* dimension within the 'increasing' body of the Antichrist still 'harboured' in the Church? Is the contradiction at the heart of the *ekklesia* at the same time a conflict in the ranks of the Antichrist? Read in the light of the figure of the *katechon* these dramatic passages of Augustine acquire an even greater significance.

The more the protagonist of the eschatological conflict is examined, the more complex and problematic it appears. We have seen how difficult it is to assimilate it to empire. If the fourth beast of Daniel is interpreted as an image of the Romans then it is clear that nothing in the power of Rome could restrain the Adversary's momentum as Hippolytus inconsistently maintained.[4] If indeed Rome extolls its force of law and right – however unjust when applied against the Christians – in an effort to reduce it to the *katechon* (which seems very much to be Tertullian's position, even

---

[4] On the catechontic theme in Irenaeus and Hippolytus, see M. Rizzi (2009).

in his anti-Marcionite guise) then its power cannot be defined as truly imperial. The vision of *Romans 13* seems to relate to the general problem of the necessity of political power and not to this or that form of it – and it is clear that Paul is also thinking of an eminently bureaucratic and administrative authority with which the Christian could and should live in peace (as with the enemy!). That it was possible on the basis of *Romans* (or any other early Christian text up to the fourth century, in my view) to think in terms of the sanctity of political authority became the *monstruum* of Restoration theology.[5] For the Church Fathers *diakonia*, *servitium* (care and service) are essentially considered within the horizon of a 'juridification' of the Political and the *neutralization* of its *auctoritas*. In the end, the emperor is reduced to the figure of one who reigns, a mere *rex*, a '*servus servorum Dei*'.[6]

---

[5] The highest 'meridian' to which this idea of power can 'logically' attain can be found in Donoso's *Letter to Cardinal Fornari on the Errors of our Time*, as well as de Maistre's *The Pope* (1819).

[6] Servant of the servants of God, one of the titles of the Pope (tr. note).

V

Excursus: 'Render unto Caesar . . .'

The assumption that the problem of the connection with political power can be resolved simply by highlighting the *difference* [between God and Caesar], as the old liberal theology used to do, does not stand up to the exegesis of *Mark 12: 17*, or other similar passages in *Matthew* and *Luke*. The entire patristic tradition leads to a very different *polemical* reading of this passage, one in which perhaps more 'violently' Jesus appears as a sign of contradiction far from any concession to idle irenicism.[1]

An initial interpretation of Christ's words might sound like this: obey Caesar up to the point that Caesar demands of you such things as will not harm your reverence for God (*in nullo modo pietati nocent*). If you are asked for a tribute, give it – for

---

[1] On the interpretation of the reply of Jesus, see M. Rizzi (2009). For an interpretation seeking to moderate the power of the passage from the Gospel, see J. Ratzinger (2008).

your action will have no negative effect on your *pietas*.[2] You must be able to distinguish between a *Caesaris tributum*, a tribute to Caesar and a *Diaboli tributum*, a tribute to the devil. Satan demands a tribute that contradicts reverence owed to the Lord, Caesar does not. Caesar asks only for the *nummus*, for coin. What cannot Caesar possibly demand? That which is of God and from God, and thus Caesar can demand neither the body nor the soul nor the will. The tribute owed him can only be paid in *aurum*, in gold. *Nomisma Caesaris in auro est*. Such is Jerome's summation concluding the entire hermeneutic tradition preceding him.

Caesar *is represented* on the coin – and the representation must always be connected to what it represents. The coin *represents* Caesar and so you don't so much give as give it back to him. It belongs to him. But where do you find the image of God? The thing on which God *represents* himself, that you must return to him. And this 'thing' is the whole human, body, soul and will. To Caesar *nothing but* gold, the *tax* we must pay for our lives in this world. Necessarily of course for with coin you acquire necessities (*necessaria*). Not only is there no abstract asceticism in Jesus but the asymmetry affirmed here is a radical one: to Caesar only that which means *nothing* to either the spiritual dimension or the human body and will. Give unto God the *human being*: The human is the image of God. God's image is figured in the human (*Dei autem nomisma homo est. In homine est Dei imago figurata*).

---

[2] In the New Testament the Latin term *pietas*, which originally meant 'duty', came to denote a special kind of reverence towards God (tr. note).

Unto Caesar not even the body – only what materially nourishes it. Caesar is needed only to sustain the body. The *living body* is from God and unto Him we must return it, together with the soul and the will. However, even here we do not reach the highest level of asymmetry; this consists in understanding 'to render unto Caesar' as a radical *renunciation* of everything that is Caesar's. Paying the tribute no longer appears as the fulfilment of an obligation or a duty but as a *liberation* from everything in us that is not *imago Dei*, in God's image. First Origen and later Ambrose interpret the passage from the Gospels in the light of 'leave everything and follow me'. *Aurum*, gold, is a burden, an *impedimentum*. What must be nothing to you give to Caesar. He only has power over that which for you is *nothing*. Only a faint line separates this statement, in which the idea of power is hollowed out, from the annihilation of the bearer of power.

Far from finding in the passage from the Gospels the basis of a peaceful arrangement, Origen and Ambrose exalt its *mystical* dimension. The human being is the image of God but has also committed sin – and since then the original image is in conflict with another stemming from the Enemy. 'Render unto Caesar' comes to signify not only freeing yourself from all *religio*, all obligations, to him but also *deposing* the image of the Enemy who still marks you. That is to say, lay aside all that still inclines you to *malevolence*. To return the coin to the one who is represented on it is the 'image' of the will finally to renounce all that binds us to the true *prince* of this world. If you do not give up the *nummus*, the coin, you can never express your being as *imago Dei*, as the image of God. Still, this *translatio* is required:

on the coin Caesar's effigy ultimately appears as the mask, as the *persona* of the Enemy himself.

The spirit of the Gospel account seems to accord with this interpretation. To the question of the Scribes 'whether' the tribute should be paid, Jesus responds just as though they understood neither his preaching nor his *deeds*. Do you not see I have left *everything*? Have you not heard that those who follow me are called to abandon even their mother and brother? And yet you want me not to abandon, not to *reject* what is Caesar's? Not only my soul but my body and will are absolutely alien to Caesar and to his State. Caesar asks me for a coin? Here it is – it was always his and I had already freed myself of it. I do not in the least contest the authority of Caesar in this field. Indeed, I fully acknowledge it precisely because it has nothing to do with whom I obey and whose part I am.

However, the dilemma arises because Jesus neither says that the image on the gold coin is that of the Enemy nor does he simply show ignorance of its 'value'; he just wants to give it back to Caesar. Implicit here is the recognition of Caesar's function as guarantor of *necessities*, the recognition of his *servitium* and just as much perhaps of his function as already a barrier to evil. But *this* Caesar is simply *impossible* – even more impossible than the love of Jesus. Power could not be reduced to such a minimal catechontic form without disappearing. A power that is pure service is no longer power and could not continue to reign if every link with the *will* of its *cives* were to be broken. A *katechon* without a soul is perhaps conceivable but not without a body and a will. This indeed seems to be the meaning of the Word of Jesus.

Faced with the question of the scribes, he does not simply repeat that his kingdom is not of this world, he does not merely 'look and pass on'[3] but listens and responds. He lives in the city and knows who Caesar is – and it is here at the very heart of the city where he forcefully poses an irresolvable problem. On the one hand, do not fight political authority – for to fight means to reinvigorate it[4] – and on the other, empty it out from within, divest it precisely of all its *auctoritas*. That is, on the one hand arrive to a point where its image borders on that of the Enemy, and on the other demand it, so to speak, in the bare form of *servitium*. It would be easy to escape the dilemma by conceding that the gold coin *also* has soul and will – and, conversely, it would be easy to escape it by 'absolutizing' the Kingdom, as if it were not written 'thy will be done on *earth*'. But to follow the paradox of Jesus 'is the task where the mighty labour lies' ('hoc opus, hic labor'[5]).

---

[3] Dante, *Inferno*, Canto III, 51.

[4] This is my summary of Karl Barth's position from the first edition of his Commentary to Romans 13 (1919). See Karl Barth, *The Epistles to Romans* (1968).

[5] lit. 'here is the task, here is the hard work', Virgil, *Aeneid*, VI, 129 (tr. note).

VI

The Church and the Katechon

It is evident that the present enquiry returns to the heart of the problem of the *katechon*. In its light the latter appears as the difficulty of a particular praxis that must at once hold to the demands of *servitium* with regard to *necessaria*, to building a barrier against *anomie*, to recognizing fully the primacy of the spiritual. Consequently the *katechon* must take the form of a complex, organized power but not that which belongs to empire nor that which belongs to the Church. Furthermore, if the *katechon* also has a mediating role, it will recognize the claims of political power just as much as the testimony of those who have received 'the love of truth'. But to what extent is this possible? It is clear the power the *katechon* wields is not mere fiction, it is equally clear that it proves infinitely weaker than the power of the Adversary, and while its function is essentially and ineluctably linked to the testimony [of the believers], its practical use is in doubt: must it not ultimately be taken out of the way? All *medietas* is destined to collapse in the apocalyptic hour. Can the *ecclesia militans*[1] the church militant, be eternal? And if, as it seems, the *katechon* occupies the position of the middle *in this time* (*nel secolo*) playing a role of temperance and moderation, then it must also have special affinity for those who expectantly wait in *spe* (hope) for the *novissima* (the Last Hour) and for that reason it *will want* to be taken out of the way.

Why a withholding power? The ambivalence it generates seems insuperable. In its struggle to contain the *Antikeimenos* (that is, the community of the Antichrist) it appears to stand clearly on the side of the righteous but up to what point? Its role could just as well be seen as an attempt to sustain the energy of the Adversary, knowing well that the *pleroma* of the latter will coincide with its own destruction. Would this catechontic activity consist then in extending as far as possible the moment in which the Iniquitous is allowed to manifest himself as *energos* (in all his energy)? Will catechontic opposition eventually turn into an assisting of the will to endure (assuming that this is indeed the will of the *Antikeimenos* – rather than to rush to its *own end*)? Catechontic *praxis* then would be a prime *exemplum* of *heterogenesis* of ends. It will amount to an admission that all opposition within the domain of the Prince of this world is destined to turn into a contributing factor to his will to power. Only faith in Jesus who is the Christ, faith upon which the firm

---

[1] As one of the divisions of the Christian Church, the *Church Militant* refers to the Christians who live on earth and fight against sin and evil. The two other major divisions are the *Church Triumphant* (*ecclesia triumphans*) and the *Church Penitent* (*ecclesia penitens*) (tr. note).

hope in His coming is founded, delivers us from evil (*libera nos a malo*), whereas any withholding power opposing the advance of *anomie* will not only become an integral part of the latter's history but it will also drive its force to greater violence, like a river that has burst its banks.

The *katechon* cannot fail to participate in the most intimate fashion with the principle it strives to withhold and delay, if not bring to a halt. It is impossible not to *retain* what you seek to *contain*. Every catechontic power must constitute itself within the dimension, even the cosmic dimension, of the principle of *anomie* that is destined to triumph. Evidently, the former could not be derived from the latter since both powers are expressions of a plan that transcends them, a plan that makes history into the ultimate *test* whose purpose is to arrive at a clear-cut separation between those who believe in the true and those who believe in the false. However, even while the *katechon* opposes the Adversary it cannot fail to preserve the latter's energy and postpone his eruption – we have seen this in its most 'diabolical' form in the 'retention' of the numbers of the Antichrist in the Church.

Conversely, one could also argue: it is by reason of His *mercy* that the *katechon* works *as if* the day of the Lord could be deferred or even never happen. It is not only political and civil authorities (*exousiai*) in their role as true *defensor pacis*, defenders of peace, but also spiritual authorities who, though aware, even if naively, of the appalling sufferings necessarily preceding the *parousia*, could end up acting in such a way as *not to see* them. Who could bear the violent upheaval when the blood of the righteous will be shed, children killed in the latrines and the cemeteries of the saints desecrated (Hippolytus, *Commentary on Daniel*, IV, 51)? The *katechon*, fully aware of the inevitability of the End and in possession of that faith which grounds the hope for it, may find the advance of destruction and ruin, of *anomie* and *apoleia* intolerable and out of love for mankind (*philanthropia*) rise against the Adversary. It is on this basis that the Church will recognize the 'good' function of imperial power. And it is according to this scheme that the Son of Perdition turns into the *barbarian* and the universalism of imperial law is providentially wedded to the evangelizing mission; thus empire and the Church jointly *hold the form* of the Age in vigilant expectation while quelling the pride of impatience. Is this not the model of all 'holy alliance' between political power and the Papacy?

This irenistic and conciliatory philosophy of history has been endlessly repeated in various ways; however, it holds only if the aporias we encountered so far are not taken into account. In fact, if authentic catechontic power is only conceivable as an internal dimension of empire, it will inevitably come into competition with spiritual authority. Were the empire to be conceived as the *enemy* of the Adversary, no exegesis of the apocalyptic tradition from *Daniel* right up to the *Apocalypse of John* would carry any weight. If we confused *anomie*, which is the spirit of the Iniquitous, with *anarchy* or reduced it to *barbarism*, we would be misunderstanding its structure and missing its importance. The Adversary does not attack from the 'outside' like a foreign invader! He emerges *from* the Age that bears the name of the Son – indeed, even from within the bosom of His Church. Even more, he emerges from that imperial power which providentially prepares the world for the universalism of the gospel of the new Covenant. If opposition to him is to be effective, the *katechon* must seem able to oppose itself to all the powers of the Age, or at least, to those intrinsic aspects of them through which they participate or are forced to participate in the power of the Antichrist.

The 'history' of the Antichrist is made up of edicts, laws and kings; he wages wars for dominion not rapine. They who lament Babylon, the kings of the earth, the merchants ('*emporoi*'), the great merchants, in the end, 'shall see the smoke of her burning', for no one buys gold and silver, fine linen and purple, ivory, brass and iron anymore. It is the wrath of God (*ira Dei*) that destroys 'all magnificence and splendour' (*Rev 18:9:19*) not the tents and carts of the barbaric hordes! Moreover, the Adversary is well aware that the empire must also be a consummate spiritual power. Far from revealing an anarchic drive, the realm of the Adversary combines sword and altar and for this reason he must *rise* like God and *found* his own cult and following. The Adversary is not an anarchist but an *apostate* and apostasy, the *ordering* of apostasy, is on the whole a civil, political and religious fact. It is undoubtedly *anomos* but only with respect to the law of Christ, that is, the *foolishness* of the preaching of the Cross (*1 Corinthians 1:18*). Could imperial power fail to contain within itself this *anomie* without being forced to express it violently? And how then could it be a *katechon* in this regard? Only in the sense that it contains *anomie* within itself, in the sense the latter constitutes its secret. If expressed in its fullness the conflict with the *ekklesia* would be unavoidable – and its outcome prescribed. For the kingdom of the *Antikeimenos* to last, it is necessary that the power of imperial order – which cannot fail to be also spiritual order – 'guard' his spirit, veil or re-veil without ever completely unveiling it. In this way, Adversary and empire could interweave their destinies without confusing them. But could Church *and* empire be able to do this – and precisely by means of mediation reach a catechontic compromise?

The charisma of the Church consists entirely in the proclamation of the Kingdom – or even in its actual proximity, its being-here-and-now and in every instant for those who believe – and hence in preaching *now* the radical *conversio* of the human. What could this mission have to do with that of the *katechon*? The *katechon* acts only in the face of or perhaps, as we have seen, within the power of the Antichrist. Will the Church confront this problem only negatively – on account of the antichrists it harbours within it? Is it in order to offer a line of defence to their number and act as a barrier against them that it too has to take on a catechontic dimension? But then this is true for every worldly power: for the empire too must contain and arrest the forces that undermine the full realization of its own nature, a nature that bolsters the will to grow, to secure and expand its dominions (and for that reason appoints itself a spiritual *auctoritas*).

The catechontic figure appears increasingly as an ensemble of actors (*personae*) who, putting on different costumes, perform in different scenes, now appearing decisively political, now religious, now as imperial officers, now as church servants (*diakonoi*) and ministers (*leitourgoi*). All the while, the ambivalence of its power grows more radical: keeping the empire from confusing itself with the Adversary and preventing his rapid rise; confining within the Church the numbers of the antichrists, who are not 'of us' and keeping the latter from waging a decisive battle against the empire or from reaching a *verdict* regarding its character. In addition, the *katechon*, as said above, can pursue an autonomous character (although far less meaningful than before) by representing itself as the bureaucratic-administrative State or 'police'. The Church can always be tempted to lend support (*avvalorare*) to its 'weak' image – an imperial idea, a 'grand politics' is likely to assume the colour of *aion* and for that reason compete not only with the form of ecclesiastical rule (*hierocracy*) but also with ecclesiastical rank and honour (*tîmê*).[2] But a *katechon* that is not properly active (*energos*) through its membership in and familiarity with the two principal politico-spiritual domains is a pure *fiction*, a will to powerlessness. Therefore the Church, to the degree it views catechontic energy as indispensable, will seek to compromise with 'strong governments', while being aware, with the political realism that distinguishes its entire tradition, that nowhere on earth will there ever be empires which will peacefully *obey* those who believe their charismatic authority to be the expression of the End of the Age.

The more settled and powerful the epoch of the Political appears to be, the more *prized* its *nomos*, the sharper will be its

---

[2] On political and clerical power, see the relevant passages in Max Weber's *Economy and Society*.

contradiction with the Age. The *katechon* remains agnostic regarding this eschatological discord – or else seeks to lessen its impact. In this respect it is active *within* the two realms or, as they are often called, the two cities (*duo civitates*). In the first realm, whose relations with the *Antikeimenon* are abyssal, it is a question of putting reasons 'calculated' to securing its own continuing survival over the *libido dominandi* which is its characteristic feature. In the second, it will have to place the universalistic demands of its own mission (which render it 'homogenous' with the imperial vocation) over the eschatological preaching for which no worldly power is 'justified' in confronting the Enemy, unless it can openly confess that its hope is founded on faith, 'whosoever acknowledgeth the Son hath the Father also' (*1 John 2: 23*), something which would ultimately amount to a recognition of the primacy of spiritual *auctoritas*.

The figure of the *katechon* is delineated as a place of progressive splittings that take place not only between empire and Church but also within the imperial sphere itself, between those who restrain the impetus of the Adversary and those who restrain the monotheistic 'anti-trinitarian', theological-political instances of the Church,[3] and also within the Church itself, between those who refrain from a compromise with Rome and those who

---

[3] The obvious reference is to the famous essay by E. Peterson, *Monotheism as a Political Problem* (1935; 2011), where it is stated that compromise with political authority, understood in the most radical sense as empire, is not available to a trinitarian theology. The present work aims to show that the relation is more complex. It aims to show the exact way a trinitarian theology can develop all those forms of catechontic power in their necessary dialectical entanglement for the constitution of imperial form.

contain the definitive 'emergence' of the antichrists. An equivocal figure, an *in-secura maxime*, an utmost in-security and thereby characteristic of the Age, of the *nunc-et-nondum*, now-and-not yet. A figure composed of *simulatores*, of dissemblers who simulate the will to power but actually aim to contain its expression, who pretend to confront decisively the *Antikeimenos* but who in reality must join him, who simulate solidarity with the forbearance of the Church but whose resistance is really a sign of the compromise they pursue on the one hand with the earthly powers and on the other with the Adversary himself. *Larvatus prodeo*, I come forward masked.[4] Dissembling is not deceiving, it is pretending (in all the senses of this word) to possess power that in reality you do not have. Only when the *katechon* wants to raise itself up to the level of autonomous energy does its activity turn into pure deception. If the *katechon* is to have any autonomous significance, it will have to assert not only the end of the two great contending forces (or the meaninglessness of their confrontation) but also that there is neither epoch nor Age and that time does not manifest an eschatological character but is merely interminable, indifferent duration over which *logically* the Prince of this world wields absolute power. Were the *katechon* to reveal a *nomos* of its own in order to silence the other powers, its figure would turn into a perfect imitation (*simia*) of the Adversary. If the dominion becomes that of the *katechon*, the advent of *anomie* would be inevitable qua *apostasy* and dissolution of the *order* secured by the empire.

---

[4] The phrase belongs to René Descartes (tr. note).

All these possibilities *symbolized* in the figure of the *katechon* need to be carefully weighed together. Each exists for the other by virtue of their conflicts and reciprocal compromises. To abide in the end-time it is necessary that the dominions be reciprocally limited – each of which would wish to be *universal* – and that each in some way comes to recognize the claims of the other. The *katechon* is the space of such mediations, including the immanent tendency of every power, shared by the *katechon*, to reduce every other to itself. A tendency that perhaps becomes more emphatic at the twilight of the Christian Age. All powers are in their turn contained in the Hour of the assertion of the Antichrist, hence their boundaries touch the essence of the latter as they draw near and risk themselves in his destiny. The temptation (*cupiditas*) to make itself an Idol pertains to the empire while theocratic temptation pertains to the Church, aware that only recollection of the End can hold the form of the Age (this is the path offered by the Accuser[5] to Jesus and so the Church could never openly admit it). The emptying out of the eschatological and messianic meanings of time and the forgetting that no power can prevail against the Son of Perdition are all elements immanent to the nature of the *katechon*. Is it possible to think this from a different perspective without stumbling over ground already traversed?

Thus far the *katechon* has been mainly understood in the form of *mediation*, even when it seemed to be at work in the Church confining and 'guarding' the antichrists. But the other

---

[5] One of the disguises of Satan in the *Book of Revelation (12:7–12)*, also the *Book of Job 1:2*.

side of its acting *as if* the Last Judgement could be delayed might consist in *pleading* that *more time* be granted so that the *infantes*, the new born,[6] may become *gregoroi*, watchful that *more time* be granted to the heirs incapable of receiving the Logos that they might turn to Him. Where the force of deception is at work ('*energeitai*') this *faciaes*, this feature of the *katechon* is employed in the desperate hope of prolonging the End-time – not in order to allow the overwhelming advance of the Adversary, nor to let the empire expand nor to let ecclesiastical order claim spiritual monopoly, but in order to make the 'stubborn' receptive until they are open to the love of truth. This pleading prayer is a *delaying force*, like Abraham's prayer upon the imminent destruction of Sodom and Gomorrah. It is the 'seed of the Christians' as Aristides and Justin the Apologist would say. Woe then to those who persecute Christians! Rome must understand that to silence this cult, should it ever be possible, would mean precipitating the dissolution of its own empire.[7] Theodore the Interpreter and Theodoret of Cyrus view the *katechon* along the lines of an intrinsically evangelizing Christian preaching, for if the gospel of the Word has to reach all peoples it will have to survive all persecution. It is only when its purpose is accomplished that the full apocalypse of the Antichrist will come to pass.[8]

---

[6] *1 Peter 2:2*, 'Like newborn infants, crave pure spiritual milk, so that by it you may grow up in your salvation' (tr. note).

[7] For a 'guide' to the relations between the Roman Empire and Christianity from a socio-political standpoint, see P. Siniscalco (1996).

[8] The interpretation of the *katechon* as the gospel of the Word of God is an idea that precedes Calvin's exegesis, *contra* Schmitt's view in 'Three Possibilities for a Christian World View' (2009).

On this view, the Church itself appears as essentially catechontic, working on confining *anomie*, unceasingly calling for conversion in preparation for the 'death of time' that will come like 'a thief in the night'. The Church knows that the full realization of its work coincides with the revelation of the Son of Perdition, 'according to the force of Satan', but it also bears witness to the breath issuing from the mouth of the Lord that shall destroy the kingdom in a 'great moment' and when those who were able to resist deception shall be saved. Therefore, in spite of everything, it is necessary tirelessly to invoke *metanoia*, repentance, to labour in the vineyard of the Lord. Apostasy is not the very last but the last of the historical moments, the conclusion of the Age and the terrible, the anguished spasm of *dying time*. The *possibilities* of time burdened with suffering, discord and misery flow into apostasy, like a river flows into the ocean, but there too they are undone. And *hereafter* and forever there is what the Gospel says: the *im-possible* of eternal salvation, of which the Kingdom *now* is the living image, for those who, like the thief on the cross, believe *now*.

The Church has always maintained this apocalyptic idea throughout the history of its confrontation with the earthly powers. It is not possible to order or hold 'in form' the *natura vulnerata* of human existence unless political sovereignty orients itself towards this idea. Explicitly or implicitly earthly powers must regard themselves as functions of the general *conversio* through whose *grace* the Church strives. If they contradict it, or even just assume an agnostic position with regard to it, they will cease to count against *anomie*, and also lose their political effectiveness. In principle, and by virtue of a general law that for the Church is divine, worldly sovereignty will be that more effective the more it can appear 'contained' within a spiritual dimension and the more it knows how to show itself as *ministering* to those ends manifest in it. To the degree the Church restrains vulnerable human nature from falling prey to deception it is *katechon*; equally, it is *katechon* with regard to political sovereignty when it forces the latter to recognize it *represents* ends that transcend sovereignty; and finally, it is, as we have seen *katechon in its own right* because it knows that in its state of *peregrina*[9] *et militans* it cannot but partake of the energies of the Adversary. For all these reasons the Church is the *katechon* of the end-time, praying it might last until its own work is concluded – the conversion whose testimony had been entrusted to it.

The neat separation between worldly and spiritual power, the conception of theology itself as immanent critique and, furthermore, the demolition of every possible political theology (Barth) seem, accordingly, completely unrealistic, 'disembodied'.[10] However, equally unrealistic is their peaceful coexistence. If the Church as community 'in prayer' has a catechontic function then its own symbol must be politically representable, not simply in the forms or 'figures' of a cult but in its relation/conflict with worldly sovereignty. The 'compromise' with sovereignty necessary

---

[9] *ecclesia peregrina*, pilgrim church, is a term from Augustine's *Civitas Dei* and it denotes the earthly historical pilgrimage of the celestial *civitas* (tr. note).

[10] G. Lettieri's (2002) work on Augustine's political philosophy and philosophy of history moves along these lines.

to hold the form of the Age will inhere in this very symbol. The Church can radically (*radicitus*) 'justify' only those forms of power capable of exercising authentic catechontic force over the *anomie* always at work that no human energy could *overcome* by itself, and which is destined to become manifest in the general apostasy. Any self-referential exercise of power, any containment or arrest of the dissolution of the political that does not lead back to the idea of *conversio*, any attempt to prolong the end-time not ultimately conceived to permit such conversion cannot appear other than an 'accomplice' of the *libido dominandi* of the Adversary. It will also turn out to be politically ineffective since a spiritually uprooted worldly empire can only accompany the advance of the Adversary.

If there is a *katechon* which can hope that its own hope is not unfounded then this will be the Church. It is the faith which dwells, to the degree that it does, in the Church that confines the Enemy (as Hildegard of Bingen believed) and the empire's own duration depends on it. Rome might be 'reformed' and not 'completely destroyed' (*totaliter destructa*) only thanks to the Christians' plea for divine mercy; it is for this that the 'eternal city' will be spared the fate of Sodom (Augustine, *Sermon 397*). However, it is just as clear that Peter did not die for the salvation of her temples, her idolatrous effigies and theatres (Augustine, *Sermon 296*), and it is certainly not for the 'beauty' of the world that God listens to the prayers of those who call upon Him *for more time*. The full meaning of the eschatological Age that the sign of Christ inaugurates can be none other than universal peace, the peace He grants only to those who have faith in Him.

The *eschaton* of *Romans 9:11*, that is *resurrection*, life's triumph over death, signals primarily the end of *stasis*[11] between Church and Synagogue,[12] where casting off (*apobole*) the latter permits 'the reconciliation of the world' and the conversion of the Gentiles by the preaching of their apostle. Only such prayer 'justifies' and renders catechontic power effective, even if it is impossible to regard it in exclusively religious-spiritual terms. The universal preaching of the gospel is already historically implicated in the universalism of the empire. The Church cannot be *ecclesia* 'incarnate' other than in the city where contradiction persists, where the Iniquitous is at work (*'energeitai'*), where all the worldly powers with intrinsically catechontic characteristics at once conflict and converge with him, where the *stasis* persists between the holy root that bears the fruit of Israel[13] – that can never be repudiated – and its branches: terrible sign of the *not-yet* (*nondum*) whose denial would commit the ultimate sin of impatience. In other words, if the Church claims to be superior in 'holding the Age in form' then it must implicitly admit that it cannot lack catechontic power and therefore be as 'rich' in

---

[11] *stasis*, an ambivalent term, it means immobility, repose, rest, arrest, but also unrest, strife, insurrection, revolt, civil war. See also *Mark 15:7* (tr. note).

[12] This forms the eschatological background to E. Peterson's (one of Schmitt's opponents) *Die Kirche aus Juden und Heiden* (1933), on the problem of the relationship between monotheism and political sovereignty. The contradiction consists in the fact that the church professes to be universal, catholic, while 'containing' in itself only a part. It must represent itself as *the* people while not being able to 'contain' other than *a* people, in the hope that it will not disperse before the full realization of the promise. Once more the catechontic dimension of the Church comes to the fore.

[13] References here and below are from *Romans 11:16 ff.* (tr. note).

duplicity and contradiction as all the other worldly and spiritual powers. The *Church militant* cannot but feed on the energies waging war within the the City of Man, just as 'Christianity nourishes itself on *non Christianity*, "feeds" on the wild unchristian shoots of the growth of non Christianity'.[14]

But if, as I believe, it is impossible to unearth any interpretation of the *katechon* as the essential dimension of the *ekklesia* from the exegeses of the Church Fathers then it is just as hard for Christian eschatology to admit such a reading for reasons very difficult to surmount. The catechontic force of the Church springs solely from its profession of faith and stands exclusively in the service of preaching the gospel. It is a paradoxical *katechon* because it longs for *more time* while completely relying on the Lord's design. What sign could bear witness to the fact that the will of the Church is not a will to resist, let alone to dominate in relation to other powers, but stands solely at the service of the Word? Is it perhaps by virtue of this delay that the number is increasing of those who seize the *kairos*[15] *that* changes their mind and their lives? Does history perhaps show some 'progress' in holiness? In the very moment the Church affirms something of the kind it would betray the entire meaning of the apocalypse, becoming the first to make a 'progressivist' idol out of history. Thus far the *katechon* has appeared as the force of an '*as if*', but there is no way in which the Church can act in

---

[14] Vasily Rozanov (1977, 65).

[15] *kairos* usually contrasts with *chronos*. While *chronos* refers to chronologically/sequentially arranged time, *kairos* has a more indeterminate sense. It refers to a time span within which something happens and lasts or is completed (tr. note).

accordance with such a 'method'. It cannot even conceive the idea that the End could somehow be arrested – rather, it must show it to be *present* at every instant. The Church cannot *feign* eternal duration. The place, whatever it may be, where the Eternal is represented is not itself eternal – nor must the Eternal be conflated with a time of resisting, of enduring. An essentially spiritual catechontic force lives in the following contradiction: the more it prays to be granted the time needed for conversion, the more it declares time to be insignificant for the act of faith that alone can save; the more it hopes to be granted time enough to 'deserve' salvation, the more it confirms salvation and eternity to be *in toto* different from any idea of merit and endurance. The Church 'contains' only by showing the 'uncontainability' of Spirit. It is the power of the *katechon* that either folds back on itself or implodes.

In any case, the Church as an historical community existing *in hoc saeculo*, in this world but not of it, must relate to the political *katechon* that, reinforced by secular means, forms an epoch with respect to the overabundance of *anomie*. Thus the Church must also reflect in itself the structure of worldly organization, the very structure that through its will to power can always be 'seduced' into forgetting the eschatological-apocalyptic dimension. The *politeuma en ouranois* of *Philippians 3:20* is a real people, a multitude who live in the world. The *futurus* does not nullify the meaning of *civis*, while the limits of *civitatis*, the 'product' of the *civis*, touch the realms of both *apoleia* and *soteria*. Whoever it may be that must or ought to announce the Last Judgement, in the very moment of imploring it to be deferred, is the ultimate *katechon*. The latter shares a common destiny with the Last Judgement. All these figures appear in a non-chronological succession that unfolds according to a hierarchy of principles. The first figure to be swept away will be that which belongs to those who are simply terrified of the *eschaton* and who desperately protect their own survival. Then it will be the turn of the different political forms that the idea of empire embraces within itself, an empire which is not abstractly conceived but constituted *ex nationibus*: it will be the time of apostasy when all the peoples fall away from the empire, from all authentic *Roman* power. And finally, the *Antikeimenos* will overturn the form of the *ekklesia* itself: it will be apostasy from the faith in the Church as the real representative of Christ. The *Glossa ordinaria*,[16] a compendium of the exegetic tradition to which great Medieval authors including Anselm refer (*in omnes sanctissimi Pauli apostoli epistolas enarrationes*), interprets *2 Thessalonians* along these dramatic lines.[17] First apostasy, *secessio, discessio* from the imperial 'grand form' of Rome, the *translatio* of empire into kingdoms; second, apostasy from other imperial forms that tried to imitate her, piecing together a multiplicity of kings (*reges*); then the dissolution of monarchic *auctoritas* in the struggle for hegemony among the various individual States; and last but fatally: the secession of the majority of people from the

---

[16] *glossa ordinaria* (ordinary gloss) is a collection of interpretations, commentaries and exegeses from the time of the Church Fathers, and thereafter, printed on the margins of the *Vulgate* Bible (tr. note).

[17] For the importance of the *glossa ordinaria* for interpreting the *katechon*, see R. Lambertini (2009).

Church and papal authority which presages the radical apostasy incarnated in the Antichrist. The unity of the empire *and* the unity of faith in the Church will have to be eliminated in one fell swoop for the apocalypse of the Iniquitous to come to pass. A whole tradition from Ambrosiaster to Bruno of Certosa speculated on the *novissima* along these lines. When the political and spiritual forms become *comuni* then the time is ripe for the great disaster. In the kingdom of the Antichrist iniquity will be commonplace and the remains of Israel will confess from out of the depths of their desert their willingness to salute the *pneuma* of the Lord.

For this exegetical tradition the catechontic powers *simul stant, simul cadunt*, stand and fall together.[18] Their entanglement forms that dimension of the Age that stands *versus-contra* the affirmation of the Antichrist. He will come to pass neither before the dissolution of the empire nor before the pleading prayer of the Church falls forever silent or lies forever unheard. Only the *Antikeimeno*s appears without any catechontic significance yet even he is not a stranger to the fate of the withholding powers, and not only because he too expects them to be swept away. In fact, the way these powers present themselves depends on their

---

[18] This seems to be also Tocqueville's point of view. The new conserving party will not be sufficient to resist the levelling force of *homo democraticus*. The political *mores* could not by themselves *contain* the 'wicked' idea of the complete independence of individuals. Compromise with the Church is unavoidable – such will overcome the *great political evil* which for him is the clash between civil power and religious authority. The political theology of the *katechon*, as one can see, underlies all his discourse. For more on this, see the beautiful critical biography by U. Coldagelli, *Vita di Tocqueville* (Rome, 2005).

actual proximity to the Iniquitous. It is quite possible to believe that one can resist him, can contain him by yielding to his compelling force, or by wearing him down during the time of waiting, or by imitating him thereby assuming his likeness. And thus empire can show itself as an idol, in the form of the Idol that does not admit of any other cult but its own to the point of conflating itself with the *nomos* of apostasy. And thus the Church, despairing of the meaning of awaiting, and despairing of a humanity awaiting in anguish conceives of its own 'empire' without end, turning *its* own word – that it can efficiently contain and restrain – into *the* Word. In this way, Church and empire by virtue of an always open possibility immanent to them *secede* from their own missions. The most momentous sign of the advancing apostasy will not be the abandonment *of* Church and empire by the multitudes but their secession from their own missions, from the function and the faith which they ought to have embodied.

VII

The Nomos *of the Adversary*

But *who* breaks themselves against the fragile barriers of the *katechon*? Who is destined to overwhelm them? Here too the general principle takes on a specific form and can only live through a historically effective self-representation. Is *chaos* the Adversary? Clearly not, as we have seen above, in the sense of the return of an original *chaos*, the disintegration of every form in a kind of *ekpyrosis*[1] from which, *ab integro*, a new Age may begin. The figure of the 'mortal God' which contained all individuals equally within itself is exploded and the *power of representation*, through which the one who represents really thinks he can contain within himself those represented, is weakened – but from this crisis there emerges neither the absolute and simple absence of law and command, nor anarchy, nor the

---

[1] *ekpyrosis*: conflagration. The term was used in Stoic philosophy in the sense of 'conversion into fire' (tr. note).

prospect of a new Age. If *chaos* here cannot signify the Opening
which 'gives place to' as yet unheard of possibilities, since apostasy
puts an end to history, then neither can it be conflated with – as it
invariably is in Schmitt – the mere absence of measure, *das
Masslose*, which first Nietzsche and later Simone Weil already saw
as the essence of the Modern. *Anomie* is a new order, a new
nomos, that of the *Antikeimenos*. It is a 'society' founded upon his
triumph, lasting throughout the end-time. Its sign will be that of
the Antichrist, just as the sign of Christ created the Age in which
the epochs and catechontic powers took shape and form.

Similarly, just as the body of the 'mortal God' is formed from
the bodies of the *cives* (although body here means actual reality,
synolon[2] of body and mind, given that every individual is thought
to have deliberately assented to the pact that founds the state) so
too the body of the Antichrist is constituted by the energy of the
antichrists. Carl Schmitt holds the former to be well grounded,
rooted in *justissima tellus*,[3] being the unity of order (*Ordnung*) and
place (*Ortung*); while the latter is a universal mobilization that
tolerates no limits; the liquidation of all *ethos* that works to 'de-
substantialize'[4] all political power. But such work remains political
praxis! The energy that moves it is spurred by intolerance of any

---

[2] synolon (σύνολον), a composite whole (tr. note).

[3] The term *justissima tellus* originally appeared in Virgil's *Georgics*, line 460: 'fundit
humo facilem victum *iustissima tellus*', i.e., 'the Earth, *paragon of justice,* pours forth
an easy sustenance from the soil' (transl. Philip Thibodeau) (tr. note).

[4] G. Marramao's studies (2000 and 2003) seem to me indispensable to understanding
the decline of all organic vision of the Political and communitarian-earthly order.
Natalino Irti (2006) has examined the consequences of this epochal turn from the
legal studies point of view.

auctoritas deriving 'from above', of any 'super-ordained' command, and the law which propels his activity ever further springs from his own nature. It does obey but always obeys itself. All power hails from God, says Paul; and a divine Law (or *natura sive deus*)[5] wills the unity of command and that peace which derives from it adds the 'mortal god'. Every power 'justifies' the will to power; the limits of power are there where the *libido dominandi* can satisfy itself, responds now the *Antikeimenos*. Every State is a *fiction* in all senses of the word, without any essence of its own. All idols vanish before the extraordinary energy of this ultimate *Idol*: let each and every individual enjoy all the power *they can* without any external limit. Nonetheless, their wills are entangled[6] in the web of this idol, they all genuflect before it, they all become one and the same in it and all become an infinite multitude. This is how the body of the Antichrist is formed, as a 'society' of *last men*. They give life to the 'one flock' but it is a flock that will not tolerate shepherds because the inner 'shepherd' *dictates* from within their every movement and thought, declaring 'let happiness be according to your measure': 'What of love? And creation? Longing? And a star?'; man is complete; 'there comes the time when man will no longer launch the arrow of his longing beyond man' (Nietzsche, Prologue to *Thus Spake Zarathustra*).

What awaits the last man represented by the *Antikeimenos* is not anarchy but just its opposite: *arché*, principle and rule, the

---

[5] An inversion of Spinoza's famous dictum, '*Deus, sive Natura*' (God or Nature), to 'Nature or God' (B. Spinoza, *Ethics*, IV, Preface) (tr. note).

[6] *irretite* from *irretire*: to catch in a net (*rete*), like catching fish; also means to deceive, to seduce artfully (tr. note).

idea of representation is played out here in inverted form with regard to the figure of the *katechon*. The Adversary 'represents' the last men who constitute his body and energy, preaching their freedom from any 'representative', preaching their complete autonomy. The Adversary represents by de-constructing all representability. The order of the *Antikeimenos* must be experienced by the last man as deprived of all representative power. Being represented ends up by appearing to him as synonymous with violence and coercion, and in the end it is the idol of the Self that the last man worships. In this way, the Iniquitous rises against whatever is *katechon* even to the point of eradicating it. The Iniquitous 'represents' the uncontainable, and thus unrepresentable forces of the last man. But with this all transcendence becomes unrepresentable: indeed, even the idea that the human can only ex-ist as capacity for *self-transcendence*. It is as impossible to be made in the likeness of pure self-enclosed immanence as it is to be made in the likeness of God's supra-essentiality. The confrontation with the energy of the last man *exhausts* messianic time. There is neither End nor expectation, only repetitive satisfaction of individual appetites. The last man (the *Convalescent* in *Thus Spake Zarathustra*) *eternally returns* along an interminable stretch of time punctuated by the production and reproduction of needs. In his inhospitable individuality he is nevertheless the most dependent being imaginable – dependent on the universal system guaranteeing this production-reproduction. He lives in all senses solely *in his own net*, caught in the power of the *Antikeimenos*, incapable of lifting himself out of it. His epoch – which he claims will complete not only history but also the very species 'man' – is that of the *net* in its precise metaphysical difference from the sign of the *cross*, in its radical '*antichristicity*'. The former radiates out in a wholly horizontal manner and its 'project' consists in annulling – in the *hic et nunc* of global space – the very meaning of eschatological-messianic time. By contrast, the cross marks the unpredictable eruption of the Eternal on the plane of the *distensio temporis* (stretch of time) – an Eternal which always represents itself on this plane but also at the same time always *reveals itself*.

The last man has been 'secured' in the net where every relation seems calculable and where what cannot be reduced to calculation is simply *no-thing*. The *Antikeimenos*, his authentic figure intimated by the Church Fathers over and beyond his plebeian, diabolic-anarchic masks was rediscovered by the great Russian 'mystics' from Solov'ev to Florensky in the apocalyptic epoch of their own land, between the nineteenth and twentieth centuries, is given the name of *Placidus*.[7] He desires to be 'in peace' with every individual demand and belief. Everything which does not concern the 'apparatus'[8] of his realms is deemed a private question of 'the heart', an indifferent dream or a fantasy. The unity of this

---

[7] The *Placidus* (peacemaker) for Cacciari is one of the main attributes of the Adversary (the Antichrist, the Iniquitous). Not the opposite of Christ but an apostate. See also *1 Thessalonians 5:3* ('those who make peace ...') (tr. note).

[8] Apparatus renders the term '*dispositivo*' (from the French '*dispositif*'). The term, drawn from Foucault, refers to a whole mechanism of various structures (institutional, cognitive, physical, abstract, administrative) whose purpose is to promote, enhance and maintain power. In English, '*dispositif*' has been variously translated as 'apparatus', 'machinery', 'device', 'construction' (tr. note).

net is accompanied by 'sovereign' indifference to the 'conflict of values' – which are now *in-different* towards one another and not even worthy of comparison or immediately reducible to their *economic* meaning. Every questioning, all convictions and faith regarding the ecstatic meaning of existence must appear as nothing more than *evaluations*. The *Placidus* reverses the tragic Nietzschean question of how is it possible to live in the experience of the death of God into the question, how if we seek God can we pretend to live forever and return eternally? Responsibility is relegated to concerns with the satisfaction of one's own interests and to the pursuit of what 'matters' to oneself. Not responding to anything beyond that and regarding oneself as 'innocent' beyond this horizon is the maxim of the Last Man. There is no *obligation* – and law is only a demand for tutelage. The epochal conflicts of catechontic empires, of earthly and spiritual powers seem to melt away before the energy of this *last one*. He is the *apostate*, the figure of the definitive *secessio* from every power that presumes to resist the *Antikeimenos*.

However, the question returns: do we have to resist? And can the *katechon* really show that sign of patience and expectation upon the advance of the last man? From the messianic perspective, resisting can only mean to resist in the name of obedience to the Word. What is important is not the *when* but the *how* of awaiting. What matters is to remain vigilant, to be ready and not look back. Every form of earthly power is 'left to be' as empty at its core and essentially *im-potent*, but nonetheless left *to be* as such not fought 'anarchically'. And so this earthly power still works; its work is regarded as necessary and owed an obedience precisely commensurate with its impotence. This is a radically intolerable conclusion not only for political sovereignty but also for any form of spiritual *auctoritas* that would constitute a lasting *community* on its pleading prayer and expectation. Whatever meaning we assign to 'resisting' it is always embroiled in its time *in hoc saeculo* and this forces us back to the *katechon* in all its problematic and contradictory figures. The *katechon* is only such if he can viscerally *contain* the enemy.

He can think to contain the enemy only in so far as he understands the multitude in terms of the last man. True, the *civitas* which the *katechon* confronts is still that of stasis, of 'civil war' between values, of the friend–enemy relation where each must face the ultimate risk – but the *katechon* understands all this exclusively as a tyranny to be repudiated. He wants to reduce value to what is merely evaluated and all relation to an interweaving, a web, of mere points of view, and so reduce the risk of proximity to equality. In this work it seems that he can only understand the overcoming of *stasis* in the sense of the dominion of the *Placidus* – and that is to say of the last mask of the *Antikeimenos*. In this way he seems to herald, if not prepare, the apocalypse. Paul's Christians *bring themselves in proximity* to the Kingdom across the spasms of the end-time. The *katechon* approximates to apostasy 'securing' within himself the seed of the last man. Clearly, *potestas*, and not only in its imperial form, still has the ring of an *auctoritas* bestowed from above: the *cives* is also seen as *futurus* from a perspective which could 'open up' eschatologically. But the immanent force of the apparatus, whose law is nothing but the condition of its very own functioning, is already predominant. The difference, which perhaps marks a leap out of the Age, consists in the fact that precisely as *katechon* power situates itself within an eschatological horizon where it is forced to recognize its own im-potence, while the order of the *Antikeimenos*, affirming itself as something which cannot be transcended and thereby negating any instance of transcendence by producing the immanence of the universal law within the very will of every individual, claims to obliterate any other reference, any ulteriority.

By containing within itself the coming apostasy, even presaging it, the *katechon* works for its own death. Through the heterogenesis of ends he finds he has been 'nurturing' that seed that will sweep him away. He comes even to abhor this seed – he whose very name evokes the Age of mighty struggles between the powers 'from above', the empires, churches and the state's will to power. Yet in having to 'provide security' in the *stasis* rising up 'from below', in having to deplete this energy in every way and having to remove every sign of contradiction, his current can only issue in that final confrontation which is irresolvable by any human power. The *katechon* is as strong in containing as it is impotent in foreseeing. If he really could foresee what is to come, he would fall into utter despair. So what is it then that he cannot, in his own nature, even anticipate? He cannot anticipate that the order of the *Antikeimenos* is an efficacious order, he cannot see that *antichristicity* and *nomos* may not come into violent contradiction with one another. All he is able to read in the sign of the *Antikeimenos* is the desolation of anarchy. He sees the antichrists not as last men caught in the web of the *Antikeimenos* but as 'revolutionaries'; he fears the threat of the *exception* rather than the reproduction of the ever-same, of which this very moment of crisis is an essential element. What he cannot realize is that it is precisely the energy that conserves which most emphatically produces the last man.

VIII

The Two Cities

Two broad views confront one another in Christianity with respect to the eschatological significance of political power and its relationship to the spiritual *auctoritas* embodied in the Church. In this context the threads we have been trying to untangle so far intersect and illuminate one another.

The Roman Empire is *afflictum* but still able to *recreate itself*, as it has in the past. The empire is familiar with crisis, in fact it *is* crisis, yet it remains vital for the world. Augustine recognizes this – but in this regard nobody has urged more forcefully the *eschatological reserve* of which we have spoken above. It is not only impossible to ground the *potestas* of Rome on true theology, it is equally impossible to see at its foundation that theology of the learned, of the philosophers which we call *natural* theology (and it is always the case that '*in vera autem theologia opus Dei est terra, non mater*',[1] *De Civitate Dei, VI, 8, 1*). Stories that are unworthy of the theatre are essential to this cult. Mythical

---

[1] '. . . but in the true theology the earth is the work, not the mother, of God' (tr. note).

theology and *theologia civilis* are inseparable from one another. A complete de-sacralization of empire, then, and one not produced from without but through pitiless criticism of its own principles, and even through the words of the fathers of Rome, above all Varro,[2] who undertook to explain the significance of their own land to the Romans.

But that is not all. Not only was Roman *auctoritas* radically 'secularized' but its very claim to ground an authentic *respublica* was challenged. This radical 'secularization' leads therefore, and quite logically, to a vision of an intrinsically weak power – legitimate but powerless to constitute that socio-political bond which alone permits us to speak of the *respublica*. What can this bond be? Rome for sure *rationally* pursued the ends of peace but it was the peace of Tacitus,[3] one renewed with great effort and only by means of *laboriosa bella*, of strenuous wars through Virgilian *bellum nefandum*.[4] Even more, it is the peace of a truce, a compromised peace between implacably divided and opposed interests. External war for universal dominion and *bellum civile*

---

[2] Marcus Terentius Varro (116–27 BC) was an ancient Roman writer and scholar admired for his learnedness. He is known for the distinction he drew between political theology (the social function of religion), mythical theology and natural theology (tr. note).

[3] Publius (Gaius) Cornelius Tacitus (c. 56–c. 117 AD). One of Ancient Rome's greatest historians, he was also a senator. He is remembered, among other things, for his enquiries into the *Pax Romana* (the establishing of peace by defeating all the enemies of Rome and depriving them of the ability to resist her), summarized in his phrase 'they created a solitude (desolation) and called it peace' (*ubi solitudinem faciunt, pacem appellant*) which he put in the mouth of an unconquered chieftain (tr. note).

[4] 'nefandum', lit. 'unspeakable'. In Roman religion a war that was offensive to the gods (cf. bellum iustum, war with just cause). See Virgil, *The Aeneid*, book IV (tr. note).

are two aspects of the same tragic reality that not even the wisest regimes were able to overcome, not even a king like Solomon (*De Civitate Dei, XVII, 13*). But any legitimate talk of *respublica* requires a power able to maintain bonds of *justice* among all *citizens* – not only a justice limited to issues of distribution and administration based on the abstract and general ground of *nomos*, of law, but the justice that *renders to everyone their own*, recognizes the essential significance of every single individual and which draws *close* to each through love. Such a 'measure' is quite *impossible* for empire. The *civitas hominis*, the city of men, in the dealings among its citizens, in the laws which regulate it, is clearly a rational construct but it cannot claim for itself the title of a true *republic*. Let us call it then a *coetus multitudinis rationalis:*[5] a coming together (*coetus-coire-convenire*) of multitudes of individuals each rationally motivated by the will to pursue their own interests while fully aware of the need for the force of law to allow them to do so in safety. Is this not the way Livy himself narrated the origins of Rome? Peace is attainable by this route, but it is always the peace of Babylon: Rome is [for Augustine] *altera Babylon*, the other Babylon.

However, this expression should not immediately assume an apocalyptic tone. Augustine was not thinking of the prophesies of Daniel and their radical political-theological exegesis.[6] For

---

[5] 'an assemblage of reasonable beings', *De Civitate Dei, XIX, XXIV*. In those passages Augustine discusses the definition that should be given to a people and a republic (tr. note).

[6] For further discussion of the political-theological significance of the Book of Daniel in 20th century Italian thought see Caygill (2011) (tr. note).

him political power was necessary and all impatience with it should be condemned. But the figure of political power hollows itself out from within: 'In hac daemonicula civitate ...' (XVII, 41:2 – and let us not forget how great is the power of the demons (XVIII, 18:11): in this *civitas confusionis*, this city of confusion, there is no power able to rein in effectively greed, vanity, pride, avarice and envy. Any and every law is too weak to rule assuredly over our *natura vulnerata* – precisely what makes the law necessary until the end of time. Here it is less a matter of recognizing the potency of power than of denouncing precarity and weakness. Every one of power's affirmations prepares for a new defeat – just as every peace prepares new wars. Seemingly, this is the most drastic image of the empire's reduction to that form of the *katechon* that merely contains or withholds.

All the same – and this is why Augustine is so important for understanding the political-theological problem – the catechontic form of power is not opposed by a spiritual *auctoritas* that overcomes its limits and aporias through an abstract transposing of itself into another dimension. The two cities are from the beginning *perplexae et permixtae*, enfolded and mixed together with their histories – as they both *come to be*, that is transform themselves from epoch to epoch – and cannot but confirm their *shared birth*. Both emerge 'ex communi, quae aperta est in Adam, ianua mortalitatis'[7] (XV, 21). *The City of God* lives in the hope of God that only *gratia*, grace can satisfy while

---

[7] 'both [cities] start from a common gate opened in Adam into this mortal state' (tr. note).

the City of Man conforms to its own present time, 'in re huius saeculi',[8] but this does not entail their separation. The citizen of the future *civis futurus* inhabits the *city* common to all. He has a history here, a history that passes from adolescence through maturity to the fullness of time, one that parallels the emergence to its full potential of the *homo politicus-oeconomicus* of the Roman Empire. The citizen of the future *struggles* in this city not only against idolatrous power but also in bringing to the City of God more recruits 'from below', *tearing them away* from secular 'values'. It is impossible for the City of God *thrown* in this way into history to regard itself as free from the evils intrinsic to historical existence. The City of God is not the community of the perfect but of those who indefatigably strive to be complete (*teleioi*)[9] in accordance with the word of Jesus. This tension and longing cannot but lead to questioning, conflict and doubt – to the ever-present possibility of *falling*, clearly seen in the very history of the two cities in which there are *contemptores Dei* – despisers of God – among the blessed descendants of Noah, Shem and Japheth, and *cultores dei* – worshippers of God – among the sons of Cam (XVI, 10). In this world *all* have, in some way or other, gone astray (XVIII, 47).

Augustine's *Homilies on the First Epistle of John* shares this view: many reprobates live in the City of God without belonging to it and for as long as they are not washed up on the shore they continue to swim like fish in the sea (XVIII, 49). This means that

---

[8] 'in the reality of this generation/age' (tr. note).

[9] '*teleioi*', msc. pl. form of '*teleios*', meaning one who has reached his full end, his full growth and accomplishment, and so by extension, 'complete', 'perfect' (tr. note).

the City of God and the Church are definitely not the same. The Church is the *emergent* City of God, radically im-perfect and for this reason its border with the City of Man can by definition always be *transgressed*. Both cities are constitutively *in peril* because they are *in itinere* (on the way). If the City of Man teeters on the abyss of contempt for God, not even the City of God is *saved*, except through the eschatological promise – but nobody can say whether it is those who presently seem to belong to it that will be *saved*.

For Rome, the greatest political construction, is not the *respublica* and the Church is not the City of God. Spiritual authority, by virtue of its own imperfection, admits the need for a worldly power; but this has to be a power that is powerless to realize authentic justice and *renounces* the end that has always legitimated it, namely, that of guaranteeing *happiness* on earth, viz., *eudaemonia*. Every claim on its part to represent itself as effective *empire* – that is, to be an energy which not only governs but *commands* in the light of an end, to be an image of the meaning of the Age – all this becomes theatre, pure *show*. And the Church, for its part, by drastically reducing secular Sovereignty to mere administration and rendering it devoid of all intrinsic *auctoritas*, is forced not only to bend to the demands of compromise ('*utimur et nos pace Babylonis*'[10]) but is also drawn into the socio-political strife produced by the very void it has

---

[10] Augustine, *De Civitate Dei, XIX, 13, 16*. The earthly city can only attain to a 'Babylonian peace'. According to Augustine, 'The earthly city, which does not live by faith, seeks an earthly peace, and the end it proposes, in the well-ordered concord of civic obedience and rule, is the combination of men's wills to attain the things which are helpful to this life' (tr. note).

created by its attempt to constitute itself as political form and authority. It could not be otherwise, for it is not really possible to contain the tendency of the City of Man to pursue self-love to the point of contempt for God either through the employment of a secular catechontic power or by the literal (*sine glossa*) appeal to the Gospel. When this occurs the Church clearly faces its greatest danger; that is, it runs the risk of conflating itself with the City of Man and its rulers, or even of 'politicizing' the idea of the Kingdom.

The Augustinian philosophy of history seems to arrive at this aporia. Dante's philosophy of history will later raise an impressive response to it (Petrarch and humanism followed in his steps but with a tendency to rhetoric and with less speculative energy). For Dante the Church must strive in every way to be the perfect image of the City of God and *precisely for this reason* sovereign politics must likewise strive towards perfection – towards empire and an authentic imperial *auctoritas*. Any other kind of sovereign will in the end fail even to guarantee good administration. Meanwhile, should the Church find itself before a weak sovereign, the seduction of temporal power could prove irresistible and compel it to betray its mission and ultimate goal. The eschatological truce can only be thought in terms of two *Suns* both at the height of their splendour.[11]

Dante can only conceive the *katechon*, in the fullest sense of the term, as empire: perfect imperial power, that is to say, *Rome*. His discourse is the opposite to Augustine's, who even refused to

---

[11] Reference to Dante, especially *Purgatory*, Canto XVI (106–11), also *De Monarchia*, book III. The theme of the difficult but necessary unity between Church and Empire – the two suns – runs through Dante's philosophical and poetic work (tr. note).

give Rome the title of *respublica*. The empire of Dante governs, restrains and reins in wounded human nature; above all, it guides it towards earthly happiness which is in itself a *perfect* end. Even if there exists another end it does not detract from the 'autonomy' and intrinsic perfection of this political end. It is just like philosophical and scientific investigation which is not 'unhappy' simply because it is open-ended but is entirely satisfied, *happy*, every time it arrives at certain and evident results (this is the fundamental doctrine of Dante's *Convivio*). So we can also ask this: is it possible to pursue the ultimate spiritual end without peace on earth which is the exclusive mission of the Monarch? Dante's conclusions in *De Monarchia* remain unclear. That it is Beatrice who comes to us once we have arrived at our earthly end in the *Divine Comedy* does not imply that this [political] end remains an imperfect one; it does not imply that the empire needs a new guide to fulfil its role. In the *Divine Comedy* the imperial eagle is prominent among the major symbols of paradise, just as the emperor Trajan is to be found among the beatified. Yet in Dante and Augustine, there is the same need to think political sovereignty as a remedy for the failings of human *natura vulnerata*. But Dante's remedy for the infirmities of sin ('*remedia contra infirmitatem peccati*') cannot be a mere *solacium*, a mere palliative! Humanity requires strong medicine, an almost redemptive drug we give ourselves by virtue of reason alone. Perhaps here we can identify a theological transition from Dante's *De Monarchia* and *Convivio* to his *Divine Comedy*: indeed, in the poem reason itself (Virgil) is the messenger, the *angel* sent to guide us to the earthly paradise. We might ask ourselves is there any need for an intervention from above in order to *move* our intellect? Could we understand anything if its forms were not given to us? Do the words of Beatrice in Canto XXXIII of *Purgatory* allude in this sense to an error on Dante's part?[12] I think Dante's position regarding the rational autonomy of imperial form does not change at all, but the most painful disappointment regarding the practical possibility of its *renovation*, of its renewal, leads him to invoke divine assistance. It is a faith forged in the vortex of delusion, ruin and defeat – a *tragic* faith that in any case does not lead him to recant his own *philosophy*.

For Dante too, authority comes from above. The divine Word indeed demands that the *empire* be politically sovereign and rationally autonomous. If any 'primacy' can be accorded to spiritual authority then it can only be that of a merciful *paternitas*.[13] A 'primacy' that finds expression in the *power* of the Church to humble itself radically, to be destitute and evangelical, and that means to appear naked and impotent in the world, in other words *crucified*. In short, as *verbum abbreviatum*:[14]

---

[12] Regarding the vexed question of the 'transition' from *De Monarchia* to *Convivio*, B. Nardi's contribution in his *Saggi di filosofia dantesca* (1930) is central to the reading developed here.

[13] *paternitas*, Latin for 'fatherly care and feeling'. In the epistles of St Paul, 'patria' (πατρία) signifies the whole of the family. The idea is that of an all-loving father gathering everyone in one big universal hearth (tr. note).

[14] The term '*verbum abbreviatum*' has a long history in medieval theology. It literally means 'abridged/abbreviated/brief word' and it was used to refer to Christ as embodying, in this one Word, all that the Scriptures contain and anticipate. In this respect, St Francis 'abbreviates' the Church. St Francis' admonition to Friars Minor (*The Rule of St. Francis*, ch. IX) is that their expression should be characterized by 'brevity of speech' since 'a brief word did the Lord speak upon the Earth' (tr. note).

St Francis is the salvation of the Church. It is only by raising the cross of St Francis that the Church can also safeguard its own *paternitas* with respect to political authority. Only a Church openly confessing that it is not the City of God 'at work' and radically renouncing all earthly power will still be listened to and still have meaning within this world. Only an empire that rejects any compromise with the Church regarding the arrangements of political power will have the right to recognize the *paternitas* of the Church and thus help the latter rediscover itself. Two Suns, then, and the more they providentially guide *together* our wounded nature, the more the light of each shines in an *autonomous* way without either being confused with the other. *Plenitudo potestatis*,[15] all power to both of them!

Dante's majestic prophesy is a response to the drama playing out around the figure of the *katechon*. But if Augustine's political power without *auctoritas* cannot guarantee the security of the citizen, and if the rational end of happiness on earth can only be pursued through the form of empire, how could the one sun permit another one alongside itself? Dante exalts Rome but Rome cannot exist without its *religio civilis*. The Dantesque vision cannot withstand Augustine's unrelenting critique. Rome cannot rule without its *cult*, without its fanciful (*fabulosa*)

---

[15] *plenitudo potestatis* in Medieval canon law denoted Papal absolute power, the fullness of power that (should be) enjoyed by the Pope as the Vicar of Christ over all spiritual or worldly and civil matters (since the latter were considered subordinate to the former). Dante's *Monarchia* is a critique of *plenitudo potestatis*, arguing in favour of two *equal* powers, the earthly power of the emperor and the spiritual power of the Papacy, as both derive directly from God (tr. note).

theology, which even its own learned figures repudiated. Dante can only imagine a completely secularized empire in Christian terms. But there can be no imperial authority without a *cult of itself*. There can be no *civitas* without its *own* gods who dwell within it and guarantee its power, and among whom there was also a *deus imperator* in imperial Rome. For Dante the *Auctor*, the Author, of both these Suns of Church and the empire could not be other than the divine providence which would have them bound together in harmony; thus the empire which recognizes no authority over it on the part of the Church must nevertheless venerate the *transcendence* of the divine *Author* and can therefore never think of its own power as absolute. But who is called to furnish the 'interpretation' of the supreme Author? Who is the custodian of his ultimate Word? Clearly not the empire but the Church, which is called to renew itself precisely for this purpose. But how could this primacy of the spiritual fail to embody itself also on the terrain of historical and political conflicts? All the contradictions [of political theology] that we have been analysing so forcefully return here.

Dante is fully aware of this and his 'resolution' sounds like a desperate appeal to a theological rather than political kind of virtue. Empire and Church are representatives of the Author and must be interpreted as *nomina relationis*.[16] The distinction between these two dimensions would then have to be understood

---

[16] 'nominal relation', that is to say, their being representatives of the Author is not inherent in the meaning of Church or of empire but only possible in their relation to that Author (tr. note).

almost by *analogy* with the life of the triune God. But what binds them together without confusion is love – *caritas-agape*.[17] Hence the powers that they embody can be contained within their limits and realize their own mission only if at the same time they *love one another*. That is to say it is not enough that they are established in their respective autonomy, nor that they both be regarded as providential – it is necessary there be selfless love, *agape*, between them, if they are not to invade, overpower and confound one another. The *realism* of Augustine had already shown this perspective to be impossible, for this form of love is not at all required for the City of Man. The *realism* of Dante reveals the powerlessness of a sovereign not endowed with intrinsic *auctoritas* who is effectively reduced to the figure of the *katechon*. Augustine and Dante mark, then, the extreme points *in* the symbol which wishes to present the two cities, the Church and the empire, indeed any form of political power, as *representatives of the one above*. Dante can elevate Augustine in the empyrean because the symbol is common to both but only in as much as in this case this symbol is a unity of opposites, a *concordia oppositorum*.

Can we say then that the epoch marked by this symbol finds its conclusion in Machiavelli's *Prince*? Is there not an *Augustinian* realism at play here? And it is not only with respect to the inevitably *demonic* character of political power but equally with respect to the *natura vulnerata* of the *citizens* that this power is

---

[17] *agape*: love. There are four words for love in Greek, *eros*, *philia*, *storge* and *agape*. The latter is a key element of Christian ethics and theology (see *Paul, 1 Corinthians 13*) (tr. note).

required to guide and restrain (the tremendous difficulty of 'holding' peoples to the decision). The space of *virtus* (understood here in a tragic way and without any nostalgia for *mediocritas*) is inexorably divorced from that of *agape*. The decline of the idea of a *respublica christiana* is the condition and presupposition of even *talking about* an effective politics capable of generating the *virtus* appropriate to realizing and preserving the *State*. But can the problem of the relation between the 'catechontic' and 'imperial' aspects of the Political be resolved in this way? The art of preserving the prince's realm is very distinct from that required to conquer one. The *virtù* which holds the State-form has a different nature from one that *conquers* it. Thus the 'instigator' or *innovator*[18] (however indebted he may be to the experience of the past and its great *exempla*) has a mission, a calling, *Beruf*,[19] that distinguishes him from one who has to maintain an inherited State or one that has been acquired and added to a 'hereditary State'. Is it the figure of the Duke of Valentinois, Cesare Borgia, who incarnates the *virtù* necessary to conquer the kingdom? Is he the example of the 'new prince', the synthesis of great enterprises, practical ability and 'lucky astuteness'?[20] Is he the 'political animal', who unites the logos of

---

[18] See Machiavelli, *The Prince*, ch. VI. Quentin Skinner and Russell Price translate '*introduttore*' as innovator, and *inovare* as innovate or change (tr. note).

[19] Cacciari here refers to Weber's concept of 'calling' or 'vocation' discussed in his 1919 lecture *'Politics as a Vocation'* (tr. note).

[20] Machiavelli, *The Prince*, ch. IX (p. 34). Machiavelli discusses the case of a private citizen becoming ruler of his country (through the 'favour of his own fellow-citizens'). Among the qualities he needs to have is '*astuzia fortunata*', not only ability or luck but an ability to recognize his fortune and cleverly obtain the favour of others (tr. note).

Chiron with the wolf and the lion as theorized by Machiavelli in the celebrated chapter XVIII of *The Prince?* Is the power exercised by an authentic 'dux' distinct from that exercised by one who governs a 'civil principality', only with regard to its greater cruelty and that juvenile unscrupulousness which the *regni novitas*[21] demands (for it is the youth who can muster the required audacity being the friends of Fortune)? This judgement seems to hold for Cesare Borgia; but the *potestas* he must embody in order to be an *innovator* lacks an additional, more essential element, and the realism of Machiavelli the Secretary is well aware of this, even if he is perhaps reluctant to mention it. The calculated steps, the sophisticated strategies, the military art of the conqueror remain fragile contrivances unless they are combined with *prophetic virtue.* Conquest and radical innovation are more than techniques (*technai*) and unarmed prophets are destined for ruin. But equally, it is hard for arms devoid of any prophetic spirit or, indeed, deserted by it to prevail in epoch-making conflicts, and if they happen to succeed their reign is certain to be short and weak. Machiavelli's appeal to Moses, Cyrus, Theseus, Romulus *and even Savonarola*[22] is instructive in this respect and points to the unresolved problem of the nexus of *potestas-auctoritas.* No simple secularization of the concept of praxis can eliminate this problem, and yet every 'prophetic' posture in the space of the Political will inexorably conflict with

---

[21] *regni novitas*: newness of a kingdom. The phrase appears in Virgil's *Aeneid*, 1, 563–64, quoted in Machiavelli's *The Prince*, ch. XVII, p. 58 (tr. note).

[22] Ibid., ch. VI, p. 21 (tr. note).

that of the *sacerdotium*, the priesthood. It is only in Rome that these two dimensions were reduced to one – but this is a prospect that cannot possibly be pursued because it coincides with the decay and death of the *respublica* and of its *constituent* elements, its productive conflicts.

Machiavelli 'masked' the aporia by pretending that in principle the same arms could conquer and preserve the State. But the end is different, the means are different and, above all, the *virtus* required is different in both cases. So the centaur-conqueror who *rules* must also contain the prophet in himself. His end, then, and aim of his *libido* cannot be concerned solely with the acquisition of a *State*, with securing for himself a stable dominion which is spatio-temporally circumscribed, for he requires a platform for further conquests that are not only material in character. While the passion of empire is universal by nature, still, the empire will have to be in *itself* a catechontic power as well. Machiavelli praises Cesare Borgia[23] essentially for having brought peace to the *Romagne*, thus guaranteeing the *security* of his people. The uncompromising harshness, which is never merely 'savage', of his seizure of power and the means deployed for maintaining it are justified by this aim. So the aporia unfolds and deepens: to conquer a state or radically to change its constitution requires an extraordinary *virtus* as compared to that which is sufficient to rule it. And the same centaur capable of this ultimate feat should then, quasi 'naturally', be able to turn into this wise and prudent guarantor of the established order, 'forgetting' as it were the

---

[23] Cesare Borgia, Duke of Valentinois (see Machiavelli, *The Prince*, ch. VII).

prophetic universalism that caused him to act. The conclusion of *The Prince* does not leave room for doubt: Machiavelli's political hero is one who takes upon himself the great task, as innovator/revolutionary, and *arms* himself in order, however, to concentrate all his intelligence on ensuring that his own dominion *stands*. And this signifies knowing how to contain his very own nature! The appeal to the prophetic dimension, to its necessity for forming a *people* and therefore a *respublica* which will not implode into a mere gathering of multitudes (*coetus multitudinis*) is thus suspended here 'in a secular manner'. But that is why the knot which binds and separates *potestas* and *auctoritas*, catechontic power and empire, political *techne* and spiritual sovereignty, the space of the Political and that of prophesy remains firmly tied. A Gordian knot that from time to time can only be cut through or *de-cided*.[24] Machiavelli's realism shows that he is indeed aware of this, *unlike* his greatest 'masters' from Augustine to Dante.

---

[24] Brecht's poem on the Gordian knot – '... ah, the man/whose hand tied it, did/not lack a plan to untie it, but/his life lasted just long enough/for the one thing, the tying/and it took only a second/to cut it' – sheds an interesting light on Cacciari's view of the de-cision as a violent cut (tr. note).

IX

The Grand Inquisitor

In spite of the radical distance that separates them, Augustine and Dante share the view that political power is the remedy for the sin of impatience, the sin Paul censured in the letter under discussion. However, for an apocalyptic consciousness, which compresses the historical perspective to a moment of decision, not only the time of empire but also that of the *katechon* is in danger of being confounded with the full self-assertion of the Antichrist. But if such consciousness is truly inspired, it will also be able to shed light on the differences, tensions, or indeed on the *agonistics* that bind their destiny. Such is the glaring light that emanates from Dostoyevsky's *Legend of the Grand Inquisitor*.[1]

The Inquisitor is 'one of us' and comes from such depths within 'us' that his figure recalls the icon of a Hermit. Dostoyevsky returns to the same motif from the *Letters of John* emphasized by

---

[1] The following pages can be better understood only in a dialogue with the great but internally contradictory interpretations of this *Legend* by Solov'ev, Rozanov and Sestov; for an overview of their positions, see S. Givone (1984).

Augustine. The Grand Inquisitor's *antichristicity* is rigorous: it does not deny the historical existence of Jesus, it is not atheism nor, indeed, is it on closer inspection a critique of the relationship on which Paul insisted between Jesus and the Christ. But it is an arrogant instance of the shattering of any symbolic bond between divine and human, affirming the impossibility of transcending the *vulnus* that disempowers the existence of free being. *Antichristicity* becomes for him the condition of catechontic work insofar as it contains the spirit of *anomie* understood as purely destructive energy. For the Grand Inquisitor it is the *nomos* of the cross that inexorably unleashes this energy. That *nomos* wedges open the abyss of freedom in which the human being – an in-fant beyond help – cannot but fall. Such a *nomos* presupposes a form of existence capable of God *capax Dei*[2] that expresses itself moreover as empty duty or as longing. Or which could be embodied – if not contained by all possible means – only in the form of anarchy and finally even that of cannibalism, of *anthropophagia*.[3]

The Grand Inquisitor knows, qua disenchanted *katechon*, that no order could endure (and an order is an order *only* if it realizes itself and perdures) unless it is also endowed with spiritual energy. Man is not ruled by bread alone. The distribution of

---

[2] A being capable of relating to God. The paraphrase comes from Augustine's *De Trinitate*, XIV ('Eo quippe ipso imago eius est quo eius capax est eiusque esse particeps potest, ...'). The idea is that since the mind is the image of God it must be capable of relating to Him (tr. note).

[3] Cacciari seems to be referring to the fate of the sacraments following the separation between the human and divine aspects of Christ. To take the host once all divinity has been removed from the body of Christ is 'cannibalism' (tr. note).

bread (*distributive justice*) is without doubt the foundation of all power, but it is also necessary that the hand which gives be feared and revered, especially if it cannot be loved. (And this transpires most when it is believed that the hand that gives the bread is the very hand that creates it.) In this case the *katechon* is 'perfect' and this is the form pursued by the Inquisitor. He does not so much wish to restrain or arrest but rather to contain perfectly in himself that which he holds to be the unarrestable drive to *anomie* on the part of the multitude. He insists that the human being is a *rebellious slave* – and that he who proclaimed the capacity to be free as a power corresponding to, or coming close to duty was either lying or never really knew humanity. Thus the Inquisitor is a figure who stands even *beyond* the *catechontic*, and his anthropology coincides with that of Nietzsche's Last Man. He simulates the movement by which the *katechon* surpasses and definitively closes the option which animated him, that of containing within himself all the destructive drives with the view to an always possible *conversio*. *Katechon* here is translated into a coercive power 'opened up' to nothing because the very nature of being there does not transcend itself in the direction of anything and it is not 'redeemable' in any way. On the other hand, what is necessary for this existence, especially if one 'loves' it, is to guarantee its survival, security and peace. The Inquisitor embodies a *katechon* that has by now destroyed every mediation between people and the Antichrist – as a *katechon* that operates objectively as the perfect *revolutionary* poised to annihilate every *nomos*. Thus the Inquisitor stands on the side of the 'demons' precisely in feigning to be their most radical opponent. He represents Bakunin and the Tsar united in one person (and for this reason becomes a key figure in Schmitt's philosophy of history).

Does the Inquisitor hide within himself a story we shall never be told? Did he set out from the desert imagining he could become a *katechon* who would give humanity all the time it needed to set itself free and become an imitator of the free son '*Liber-filius*'? Has he stayed true to the promise-and-hope of redemption awaiting the Lord's *parousia*? His face would have us believe it. But in the city of *Cain* he came upon human beings and assumed the features (*facies*) of the *katechon* which must contain within itself both worldly sovereignty and spiritual power. These features are nonetheless still insecure and confined within an eschatological perspective that only a radical despair for humanity *desperatio de homine* could close forever. No atheism here, no negation of God, as if this were merely a matter of argument, but the tragic experience that the divine-humanity of Jesus, the Christ, contradicts *in toto* the idea of God and Man held by the world. To one who had been a saintly ascetic, human beings seemed by nature incapable of that freedom expressed in the divine-humanity of Christ. For him, a perfect *catechontic* destiny that could exceed the original meaning of the *katechon*, seems to be the only viable end and yet at the same time as an insurmountable wall.

The Inquisitor is not an ambassador (*legatus*) of the *Antikeimenos*, he is 'one of us'. He belongs to the Age whose highest standard is the super-human freedom that expressed itself in the Son. But to the Inquisitor this freedom has revealed itself to be *impossible* and that is all there is to it; to think of it as the *ultimate possible* would drive human action first to raving delusion and then to unhappiness. Patience must transform itself into the art of surviving and enduring. The force of the institution that withholds and contains must transform itself into a 'total' institution, that is to say one that is an end in itself. And thus the understanding of human existence transforms itself into a disenchanted despair about the possibility of self-transcendence or the ec-static character of its own nature. It is here that the contradiction explodes, for the 'perfect' *katechon* is the very one that declines and ceases to be such. And not only because it radically (*radicitus*) contradicts the meaning of the Gospel and already lines up with the Antichrist nor because it views humanity in the light of the latter, but because by excluding any ulterior dimension on the basis of such knowledge it already takes for granted the *pleroma* of the *Antikeimenos*. In short, the Inquisitor is an unwitting figure of the *eschaton*: not a figure who holds it back and is capable of delaying it but one who comes *late* and masks his own impotence by deluding himself that he possesses a catechontic energy which his own words show to be exhausted and spent.

The kiss Jesus gives the Inquisitor at the end of the story is a kiss for those who know not who they *are* and therefore are ignorant of what they do. The Inquisitor senses this and shivers, he sees he can do nothing to hold back the Last Judgement. It will come and it will sound to him profoundly unjust because the standard by which it is pronounced is for him alien to human nature and history. It is precisely the measure of this kiss which condemns him *now*. And it is 'unjust' because it is opposed to any logic of retribution and exchange, but still capable of condemning him to wretchedness.

The 'perfect' *katechon* is unaware of representing its own state of *having been*. It belongs in the 'body' of the Antichrist even though it comes 'from us'. The 'perfect' *katechon* shows this provenance precisely in wanting to hold back while acting in a way that reveals the Age is finished – that the *Antikeimenos* now stands alone before the breath issuing from the mouth of the Lord to be swept away when the Lord wills it. The *Antikeimenos* awaited this moment with absolute impatience – in contrast with those who passively and patiently (*patibilis et patiens*) believe in the image of their God on the cross. The Antichrist is in himself the arrogance that destroys all that restrains because he knows that where there is restraint there may be concealed a place for the prayer of conversion. In proclaiming the latter to be 'logically' impossible, the Inquisitor announces the definitive victory of apostasy – but also his own prior death. If the time of expectation is over then nothing remains to be contained. And those human beings, *in-fans*, who the Inquisitor claimed to protect in their wretchedness are transformed into his victors.

As principle of negation the Antichrist longs for his own annihilation. This he confesses to Ivan Karamazov. His logic is inexorable unlike that of the Inquisitor, who insists absurdly on thinking that his own moment is infinite, of conceiving himself in a contradictory way as at once *katechon* and *eschaton*, as epoch and Age, as Age and Kingdom, whereas in reality his figure stands in the *service* of the revelation of the last man whose energy constitutes the life of the Antichrist. The one 'who goes away' at the end of the great 'scene' in Dostoyevsky is precisely the Inquisitor, now the 'place' is wholly 'free' for apostasy. But being inevitably also an *apostasy from itself, a secessio* from its own will to exist, it leaves open the possibility of a Yes of which the kiss the Inquisitor receives is an image and intimation. Apostasy and the unconditioned Yes now confront one another. Whatever puts itself between them to contain or defer their confrontation is by now a mere 'has been'[4] even if the energy it emanates might still last for millennia, like the light of a long dead star.

Interpreted in this way the *Legend of the Grand Inquisitor* represents the extreme meridian of the history of the catechontic form (and is clearly not just a political form or an expression of the will to power as Alyosha wants to believe). Political theology is essentially structured in terms of a reflection on this history. The *katechon* hosts the conflict between the finitude of the Political and spiritual *auctoritas*, the patience of waiting and the idolatry of earthly institutions, of the will to contain and to give form to the potentially anarchic 'subsoil' of appetites, needs, instincts and the irrepressible nostalgia for holiness (how can we fail to perceive this in the Inquisitor?). But between these dimensions no dialectical compromise can be established, nor can they give life to any *catholica concordia oppositorum.*[5] As in Dostoyevsky there is no path by which evil can be overcome

---

[4] 'così fu' in the original. A standard expression in the Italian translation of the Bible rendering the Septuagint's 'ἐγένετο' (*egeneto*) (tr. note).

[5] A reference to the political ecclesiology of Nicholas of Cusa (1401–1464) in *De concordantia catholica* (1434) (tr. note).

by Good[6] (even if this self-negation of Evil, constrained by its intrinsic logic to annihilate itself, might appear to be dialectical in Dostoyevsky, nonetheless, this remains something purely possible), so too the various *features* of the *katechon* oppose and enter into conflict with one another without ever being able to arrive at a synthesis. There is the feature reducible to political form that competes with religious-spiritual *auctoritas* and one that tends towards a theocratic idea; there is another whose mission is to 'give time', a merciful deferring of the final catastrophe, and there is its opposite, characterized by an insuperable despair regarding mankind (*desperatio de homine*) that confuses itself with the proclamation of the advent of the Antichrist himself. Every epoch offers a specific combination that places emphasis on one characteristic rather than another, but whatever form power assumes in this Age, its character or *daimon* always ends up represented as at least one of these features. Is it in the figure of the Grand Inquisitor then that all these features find their common destiny? Is it in this figure that the catechontic powers, and with them the Age, fade into twilight?

If the work of the *katechon* could be completed and become autonomous, then we would be spared the Last Judgement. But the Last Judgement is immanent to this Age and every decision made within it retains, consciously or otherwise, its image. In the end, the very figure that would seemingly make catechontic power eternal reveals to us its total impotence. It only shows the

---

[6] L. Pareyson insists on this theme in his seminal studies on Dostoyevsky collected in *Dostoyevkij. Filosofia, romanzo ed esperienza religiosa* (1993).

growing power of the multitude that composes the very 'body' of the Antichrist. It no longer holds back anything but surrenders to this impetus. And the breath from the mouth of the Lord, his kiss, will *ab-solve* it forever. Indeed, the Grand Inquisitor has already passed judgement on himself in confessing his own wretchedness, that is to say, the failure of his own mission.

But this was a mission that could not be avoided. Oh how he would have preferred to stay in his desert feeding on locusts and waiting in solitary prayer for the end of all things (*consummatum est*)! Someone though had to assume this role and to play it out to the end, up to the point of confessing his own powerlessness, up to the point of surrendering to the Antichrist. This is the cup from which the Grand Inquisitor drinks knowingly and freely to the last remaining drop. The extreme stance of apostasy is indeed *secession* from the faith – but not the faith of the superstitious multitude of last men but of the Church itself that no longer believes in the energy of the Word that preaches the only true *miracles* of loving and being free. The last sign of the catechontic powers is this sin of despair. When they fall into it the end has already come – and the Antichrist, the antichrists divest themselves of them. They know how to give themselves their daily bread or how to demand it without praying and without acts of subservience. The *katechon* will discover that its power of containment *still* issued from the faith of being able to act from the perspective of *conversion* or the *turning* of the whole human being towards that im-possible measure of freedom for which Jesus is the icon. But the *katechon*, as such, just cannot remain faithful to this measure however much it may understand it. It cannot repeat word for word (*sine glossa*) Jesus' repudiation of the Adversary but it is forced to give life to earthly powers and to hold the age in form through compromise with its epochs. The compromise extends to the ultimate point of this immense task, one that coincides with the dismantling of faith, its shipwreck, its powerlessness to resist in the face of the hard lessons of history: the 'confession' of the death of God, but not of the abstract, rational God of theism nor of God as highest Being, the *causa causorum*, but of that God who is seen by whoever beholds his Son. It is Jesus, the Christ, who dies, it is his message – and it is he whom the Inquisitor in his wretchedness wishes had never been.

This destiny had to be assumed. The *katechon* is an inevitable figure of apocalyptic time. This time is indeed that of the Now, this time is indeed wholly included in the event of the apocalypse of the Son but included like a void, not as a temporal interval (*distensio temporis*) nor in the form of a duration but as an *instant* to be filled. The circle that makes up this ring comprises the incarnation of the Logos and its message – but the ring has significance for the void which the circle surrounds and for the shape it will receive. As Musil reminds us, the void is the essence of the ring.[7] This void is the heart of the ring, its life. Until the *eschaton* in which all those who have known how to resist and freely remain faithful to the call issuing from that void will be revealed, the catechontic powers will act out their destiny by showing themselves across the epochs, according to the diverse, even opposed perspectives we have described, in all their

---

[7] Robert Musil (1997), ch. 84, p. 401 (tr. note).

combinations. They are figures of the apocalyptic time proper to the Christian Age and they could not be conceived otherwise. They all presuppose the *novitas* of the event of Christ as well as Satan's *negation* of it. They must give birth to a political form for they all know how to resist in the flames of this contrast. A political theology focused on the *katechon* only makes sense within a Christian conception of apocalyptic time.

That there is little or no room for the *katechon* in Judaism is obvious, it simply coincides with the deferral of the coming of the Messiah. Judaic political theology expresses itself in prophetic preaching; political power and obedience to it – which must never appear idolatrous – are willed by God and it is from Him they derive their authority while nevertheless remaining a sign of the weakness of the faithfulness of the people to the Covenant, a sign of their immaturity (*infancia*). They have no connection with the coming of the Messiah.[8] The *katechon* however refers just to this coming; its mission departs from its historical reality. The end-time is *this one*; it is necessary to *decide now*. But how is one to face this decision? How to arm oneself for this time of 'exception'? Will there be time to do so? How can one be *already* prepared for the decision if no *more time* is granted to us? The dread provoked by such questions defines the catechontic dimension. It remains within the circle of the ring. Taken together these questions form the troubled heart *inquietum cor* of the

---

[8] See Gershom Scholem, '*Toward an Understanding of the Messianic Idea*' in *The Messianic Idea of Judaism* (1994). Moshe Idel's criticisms and clarifications of Scholem's thesis, pertinent in my view, are to be found in *Messianic Mystics* (Yale University Press, New Haven, London, 1998).

Age. They do not as much point to different moments as express different spaces which confront and challenge one another and which in this *agon* change form and direction.

The *katechon* knows that this *Now* is the very last one and there will be no others. However, this *Now* unfolds like an immense field of contradictions, conflicts and decisions. The *katechon* cannot inaugurate new Ages; it belongs only to this one in which it plays its role. Just as the time of prophesy is over for Judaism, so is the time when different Ages could succeed each other over the *katechon*. For the prophets time remains *full* time, the real time of expectation even though expectation essentially involves *how* each singularity relates to the Good News that is both a past Event and perpetually present. No new Saviour, no more *novitas*. The Last Hour (*hora novissima*) is none other than the fulfilment of *this* hour. The Last Judgement concerns that which will be believed, that will be said, that will be done here and now. What remains decisive is just this spasm of time or this void. What remains decisive then is the 'history' that inscribes itself in it. Such is the unheard of meaning of this 'history', the meaning of history proper to the last Age. There is no eternal return, no cycles, no indefinite 'enfuturing', not even a progress towards an end that may be abstractly conceived as a 'beyond'. The agonistic fullness of history contracts into a decision in the apocalyptic time of absolute emergency. The message looms over it, there is no more time *consummatum est*. This is all that can be expected and it is in the light of this expectation that the meaning of the *katechon* is configured.

The power possessed by this paradoxical messianism with

respect to the expectation of a future event (even if prepared from the beginning of time) is evident. Christian apocalyptic time is founded on an Event which has in itself the *already-now* or fulfilment of time. This *founds* hope. What is announced is not only hope but also the ground of that hope addressed to all, beyond all distinction of custom or ethnicity, in absolutely universal terms. This message can be for all because it is tied to a real event, a historically verifiable fact. The *parousia* does not innovate but reiterates that *everything* has to be decided in the light of the apocalypse of the Son. His is not so much a return as the ultimate manifestation of his presence. He will come like a thief in the night and it doesn't matter when. He will come like death. And that will be the *death of time*, even the contracted and abbreviated time of the Now. Time will be reabsorbed in light, will implode into luminous essence received by the Johannine God of Light. This 'new earth' will not know night (*Revelation 21: 25; 22: 5*). This new earth will conclude the Age of the catechontic battles including the last battle with the Antichrist. It will mark the insuperable limit. The field of 'history' opens between this limit and the originary *novitas* (in which this limit is already inscribed). Its meaning can be understood *a priori* precisely because it is already definable in terms of its own measure. Only within the space of this Age is it possible to think that historical time is the object of *comprehension*, to think that there can be a *concept* of time rather than simply a *historein* or record of times and events confined to the space of this Age. For within it paths are traced and events are not randomly dispersed. Because its world is not the sum of coincidences but every occurrence can and must be referred back to the confrontation among the powers of which the *katechon* is the central figure, for after all its world stands under the light of the Last Judgement and for this reason its 'facts' can be judged. And this is what explains the very work of the *katechon*. He[9] can think of withholding, delaying and arresting because he claims to *know* the meaning of the Age. This knowledge is essentially theological and every political power, wittingly or unwittingly, must participate in it.

---

[9] 'He' refers to *katechon* in its masculine grammatical form; indeed from here on Cacciari prefers this formulation, even reasoning in the *persona* of the *katechon* (tr. note).

X

The Age of Epimetheus

What happens when the *katechon*, once exhausted, nears its end and comes into 'contact' with the full manifestation of the Antichrist? What happens when the earthly and spiritual powers can no longer 'contain' the impetus of the latter, not even at the cost of adopting it in themselves? In the space of apocalyptic time the catechontic 'measure' still permitted, however weakly, to know, to remember and to foresee. It was Promethean power that made possible belief in the synthesis of time and concept, made possible the 'projecting' of history by organizing-containing energies and subjects. The *katechon* in its highest and strongest dimension belongs to this family of titans. But at the end, when, that is to say, the time of the end is completed, it is another *persona* of the same family who comes to dominate: Epimetheus.[1]

---

[1] Epimetheus, one of the Titans in Greek mythology, the brother of Prometheus. Together they were considered as typical representatives of mankind (Prometheus clever and resourceful, Epimetheus unwise and injudicious). The etymology of their names is revealing; Epimetheus literally means 'hindsight' and Prometheus 'foresight' (tr. note).

As a result, anyone who still believes it possible to assume a catechontic function must put on this *persona*.[2]

The meaning of 'political wisdom' has changed. The wisdom of the 'classical' *katechon* was, indeed, preoccupied with what was possible but without renouncing speculation on the most highest good. Its form was, indeed, interlaced with temperance and the mean *mesotes* without ever being reducible to *technique* (*techne*) as every one of its aspects reaffirmed its provenance 'from above'. In order to contain, the *katechon* thought necessary a *sophia* (wisdom) capable of representing the 'common good', one that could never result from the sum of particular interests. The latter can only fortuitously combine or coincide with one another and the ability which allows them to live as long as possible peacefully together is nothing but *sophrosyne*.[3] As we saw above, the dissolution of catechontic form originates from within itself, that is it 'comes from us'. It begins with the critique of the idea of empire, proceeds to that of every 'mortal God' and finally corrodes – logically and philosophically – the *reality* of the State, de-substantializing it, divesting it of all *auctoritas*, denouncing its ideological fictions and showing the impossibility of overcoming the absolute horizontal plane of the net of conflicts and interests. This formidable line of thought matures at the heart of the catechontic dimension where, as can be seen in a proper *theological*-political register, it reached a point of contact with the full manifestation of the *Antikeimenos*.

---

[2] Here *persona* has the sense of '*theatre mask*' (tr. note).
[3] Usually translated as 'prudence' or 'temperance'. See Aristotle's discussion of *sophrosyne* in the *Nicomachean Ethics*, 1140b: 7–10 (tr. note).

Conservative thought holds that this passage marks the victory of *chaos* and of *anomie* as *chaos*. But it is not at all so. *Anomie*, as already noted, is a *system*, is indeed *the* world system. In it any 'territorialized' order, as presupposed by the *katechon*, is simply unthinkable. What is unthinkable is a source of power that transcends immanent functionality – an *idea* on which its exercise depends and to which it appeals. The law obeyed by the last men is not imposed on them as the fruit of a sovereign decision and nor does it appear to be dictated with a view to reaching a state transcending the existing one. It must prevail purely as an expression of the 'natural' functional needs of the system, of the 'obvious' respect owed to the rules by means of which the apparatus labours away. Apocalyptic 'anomie' should be understood as the collapse of *nomos*, in the sense that the latter is still assumed within the theological-political symbol of the *katechon*, and is not at all synonymous with anarchy. *Nomos* represented what is Common or the property of no one. It is the 'good' of a historically and culturally specific community. *Anomie* indicates a time 'free' of spatial determinations, a time in which individuals do not tolerate being 'represented' except by impersonal norms which appear at the basis of the functioning and the 'success' of those powers on which the individuals recognize that their own *life* depends.

These powers, however, overwhelm the form of the *katechon*. But such form uniquely allowed one to fore-see, because it is possible to fore-see only that which, in some measure or other, is also a *pro-ject*. I fore-see only as far as I think I'm able to perform a subjectively determined action; I fore-see only to the extent I think I possess the energy to realize my pro-ject. All fore-sight is reduced to extrapolating from an actual situation once this catechontic-promethean idea collapses. Is this idea a mere ideological fiction? Perhaps it is – but as soon as it ceases to be of use any foresight *cum auctoritate* becomes impossible; the horizon folds into the limits of our gaze and with it even the simple administration and management of contradictions, of 'breakdowns' of the world-system become increasingly difficult. How is it possible to heal when any idea of 'health' comes to be lacking?

It is the victorious return of Epimetheus at the very moment his brother Prometheus thought to represent and celebrate his own triumph. Was it not said that with the end of the great European civil war, with the renewal of the victory at Actium,[4] an empire would be formed? Was it not said that it had already been forming, as the culmination of the Promethean era? That it would have been capable of containing and giving guidance, capable of both *potestas* and *auctoritas* just as potent in its technical apparatus as in its spiritual energy, deeply rooted like the ancient *nomos* and at once fore-seeing and audacious in the universality of its own projects? Thus went the story, mistaking the colours of sunset for those of dawn. The Promethean era could only affirm itself in its fulfilment – a fulfilment that it had precisely foreseen. Its titanic energy had served first to contain and eventually to demolish all that stood against the universalism of its own idea. This is the tension or contradiction that constitutes the very life

---

[4] The sea-battle of Actium (2 September 31 BC), where the fleet of Octavian Caesar defeated the combined forces of Mark Anthony and Cleopatra. It is also thought to mark the consolidation of power under a central figure, Augustus Caesar, later emperor Augustus (tr. note).

of the catechontic form: on the one hand it cannot tolerate the autonomy of the part, of the individual with respect to the whole, but on the other it harbours within itself the need to be rooted in a *nomos*, to determine or to 'individuate' itself. At the moment of its fulfilment-decline the fate of the *katechon* consists in the will to contain *the Globe*[5] within itself.

But here emerges the apocalyptic aporia. There cannot be a *nomos* of the World just as there is no such a thing as the Law of nature. There exist only *these* determinate laws. And, *beyond* these, there exist forces, decisive powers operating on a global level whose productions follow norms internal to their own function and which are by nature alien to all legislation 'from above' and cannot tolerate any *katechon*. For this very reason they are essentially unforeseeable. Not only because the complexity of the relations to which they give rise, traversing various institutional levels, rights and procedures, is literally un-containable, but also because the will of each of these forces *does not know* the global effects of its own *impetus*, effects which, in turn, prove decisive in determining its very individual figure. What each individual will 'knows' is only the quest to develop its own power for *as far as it can*. All this represents the movement which from 'below' disrupts the catechontic power. But it is a movement inseparable from the one that demolishes catechontic

---

[5] English in the original. In an interview with *La Republica* (22 May 2014), Cacciari uses the term globe to mark the decline of politics and its total submission to the economic. This state of affairs has turned *the world* into a *globe*. He also points out that the Globe was 'the consecrated symbol' of the 1889 Paris World Trade Fair (a Fair celebrating the centenary of the French Revolution) (tr. note).

power from the inside and which has been presented with its promethean features (*facies*). It is a question of two faces of the same process.

Before the destined crisis of the catechontic-promethean orders, all appeals to the Political sound like feeble rejoinders. Every political form necessarily ends up turning into a function of those same powers whose physiology cannot tolerate its primacy. We have followed this process from a political theological perspective, but one could also do so from a historical and social perspective. The Political can no longer claim any 'authority' that does not present itself at 'the service' of the function of the technical-economic system. This holds exclusively in as much as it belongs to the elites, which administer this system, in as much as it is a node of that net which they compose. Once more this seems to be in perfect analogy with the process issuing 'from below': inability to tolerate any 'personal' sovereignty', any idea or 'guide' that transcends the 'mechanism'. Everything 'holds together': de-substantialization of the economic-financial world, eradication of catechontic powers, individuals obeying only those norms which appear to them necessary for the satisfaction of their own needs, needs which are 'uncontainable' in principle.

Will this world-as-system mark the coming of the *Placidus*? Clearly not in the sense Epimetheus seems to promise – that is to say, in the sense that the 'closure' of the Promethean perspective may render possible the reduction of all conflict to calculation, and so make possible the end of the struggle for hegemony between the powers. It does so rather in the eschatological sense of inaugurating the space of *permanent crises*, of passing seamlessly from crisis to crisis with no armistice, let alone peace. The reign of the *Placidus* is the opposite of undifferentiated unity. The *elite* which governs it is far from expressing a commanding identity, an identity which only a Promethean energy directed towards an End strategically 'enfuturing itself', could render thinkable. The impersonality of the Sovereign, on the other hand, entails the affirmation of the multi-headed[6] character of power, or better, entails the continuing competition among its various functions over claims to be the true interpreter and representative of the immanent Law of the system. The shared basis of their 'vision of the world'– that is the unshakable faith in the fact that every meaningful problem must be expressed in a technico-administrative form and can only be resolved through the power of the technico-administrative apparatus[7] – far from reducing the bitterness of conflict only tends to exacerbate it. Theologically, all the forms of Epimethean power

---

[6] the word used here to describe the character of power is 'policèfalo', possibly an allusion to the beast of the Apocalypse and to the famous second labour of Hercules (the Laernean Hydra). See also Plato's *Republic*, book IX, 580d–ff. (tr. note).

[7] The critique of such *faith* constitutes, in my view, the most significant historical-philosophical core of Ernst Jünger's work, once it sheds the 'expressionistic' tone characteristic of *The Worker* (1932), *Total Mobilisation* (1930) and the later *Leaves and Stones* (1934). In my view his most important works remain, in my view, The *Gordian Knot* (1953); *At the Wall of Time* (1959), and the much later *Twice a Halley's Comet* (1987). The fact that awareness, of the omnipotence of Technique is a matter of *belief* in it, is absent in Jünger and makes it impossible for him to think the *Weltstaat*, the world-system (see his 1960 essay of the same title), as a *conclusion* of the Age. Furthermore, Jünger seems to share with Schmitt the idea that the collapse of all catechontic forms (to which the *Weltstaat* belongs) would coincide with the 'realm' of anarchy. The *porosity* of all key terms of theological-political jargon (such as responsibility, freedom, war, peace, etc.) serve as an image-portent of such anarchy.

are apostatic, but precisely because everyone affirms their individual 'freedom' and, in the end, *ab-solute* with respect to the others, precisely because not one of them can actually conceive of anything 'more' than themselves and even less tolerate being regulated or organized by anything other than themselves; in the end what results is constant competition. Nothing is more unreal than to think of the world-as-system as tightly regulated by the *arcana* of empire (*arcana imperi*) since this would be to project the image of the stronger *katechon* upon its own. If the Age of the Christian *katechon* is one of great wars and revolutions that of Epimetheus will be an Age of *insecurity* and permanent crises. Theologically speaking, this can only represent the last spasm of time before the *Decision*: its duration is politically unpredictable and as its moments become gradually ever more unpredictable as its impetus weakens until finally it destroys all catechontic regulations.

The *moment* of the *Antikeimenos* is not therefore one of a Tyranny more or less ferocious, but rather that of the growing autonomy of the spheres of power and their internal conflict in the 'light' of apostasy. The harder these diverse realms – economic, financial, political, juridical, technical-scientific – compete, the more they will share the same *Weltanschauung* (that of the world-as-system with all its structural aporias). In this competition the realms, liberated from super-ordinated regulation, can only change their configuration and their own internal normativity. Thus the ancient form of state sovereignty, the true model of the *katechon*, must 'overcome itself', relocating itself in a dimension which, on the one hand, will render it ever more *relative* and, on the other, will force it to produce these 'mighty spaces' which, for reasons we have discussed can only be weak mimicries (*simia*) of empire. The juridical norm for its part has to accommodate itself to this centaur-like artificial natural law to which we refer whenever the 'laws' of the economy or market are invoked. For the 'social brain', the producer of innovation, in turn, being stripped of every trace of 'auratic' autonomy, in order to compete effectively will have to reveal itself as a production of forms of life, as that law which structures them from within themselves.

Epimetheus cannot know either the times or the modality of these transformations. All that the *permanent crises* can today allow us reasonably to claim is that they will not give rise to new catechontic powers. It is possible that 'great spaces' will emerge in competition, 'led' by elites which while in conflict among their various powers nevertheless share an absolute intolerance towards any power whatsoever that transcends their own movement. They are united only by their shared apostasy with respect to the Christian Age. There does not seem to be much more than this to know. Prometheus has withdrawn – or has once again been crucified on his rock, and Epimetheus is at large and in our world opening ever newer Pandora's boxes.

Appendix 1

The Katechon Archive

Paul (Tarsus c. 5–Rome 67)

Now we beseech you, brethren, by the coming (*parousia*) of
our Lord Jesus Christ, and *by* our gathering together unto
him, that ye be not soon shaken in mind, or be troubled,
neither by spirit, nor by word, nor by letter as from us, as that
the day of Christ is at hand. Let no man deceive you by any
means: for *that day shall not come*, except there come a falling
away (*apostasia*) first, and that man of sin (*anomia*) be
revealed, the son of perdition (*apoleia*); who opposeth and
exalteth himself above all that is called God, or that is
worshipped; so that he (*ho antikeimenos*) as God sitteth in
the temple of God (*eis ton naon*), shewing himself that he
is God. Remember ye not, that, when I was yet with you, I
told you these things? And now ye know what withholdeth
(*to katechon*) that he might be revealed in his time. For the
mystery of iniquity doth already work: only he who now
letteth (*ho katechon*) *will let*, until he be taken out of the way

(*ek mesou geneta*). And then shall that Wicked (*Anomos*) be revealed, whom the Lord shall consume with the spirit of his mouth, and shall destroy with the brightness of his coming (*parousia*): *even him* (*Anomos*), whose coming is after the working of Satan with all power and signs and lying wonders, and with all deceivableness of unrighteousness in them that perish; because they received not the love of the truth, that they might be saved. And for this cause God shall send them strong delusion, that they should believe a lie: that they all might be damned who believed not the truth, but had pleasure in unrighteousness (*adikia*).

Second Letter to the Thessalonians, 2:1–12

Irenaeus of Lyons
(Smyrna 130–Lyons 200–02)

The Bishop of Lyons, regarded by many as the founder of Christian theology, his most important work, Against Heresies: 'On the Detection and Refutation of Knowledge So Called', *mounted a systematic attack on Gnosticism (Books 1 and 2) and an institutional defence of the institutions of the sacramental Church (Books 3, 4 and 5). Cacciari's passages are taken from Book 5 where Irenaeus criticizes the gnostic view of government as intrinsically diabolical and pursues an extended mediation on ecclesiastical eschatology (tr.).*

XXV. The Antichrist shows himself as the one who wants to be worshipped as God, being as he is an apostate and a great thief, and he wants to be proclaimed king, even though he is a slave. In fact, after having received the power of the devil, he will show himself not as a just king, and even less as God's subordinate and servant to His law, but as a wicked and iniquitous one, an apostate, lawless, unjust and murderous, as a thief who takes in his bosom all the apostasies of the devil; he would destroy all the idols in order to feign he is God, and he will establish himself as the only idol, collecting in himself all the deceptions of all other idols, so that all those who worship the devil through all kinds of abominations become his servants. In fact, the Apostle speaks of him in the *Second Epistle to Thessalonians*: 'Let no man deceive you by any means: for *that day shall not come*, except there come a falling away first, and that man of sin be revealed, the son of perdition; who opposeth and exalteth himself above all that is called God, or that is worshipped; so that he as God sitteth in the temple of God, shewing himself that he is God' (*2 Ts 2:3–4*) – therefore, the apostle has clearly spoken of his apostasy, has clearly stated that the one who will raise himself above any being considered as God or an object of worship, that is above every idol (those who human beings call 'gods', even though they are not), will thus strive to present himself as God in a tyrannical manner.

XXVIII. While in this time some turn towards the light and by faith unite with God and others turn away from the light and from God, the Word of God assigns a fitting habitation to all: those who are in the light may enjoy the goods that are contained in it, but those who are in darkness partake of its suffering. For this reason [the Word of God] decrees that those who sit on the right hand will be received unto the kingdom of the Father, and those who sit on the left will be cast into the everlasting fire (*Mt 25:34–41*), for the latter will be deprived of all goods. Thus, says the apostle: inasmuch as they have shunned the love of truth for their salvation, 'For this cause God shall send them strong delusion, that they should believe a lie: that they all might be damned who believed not the truth, but had pleasure in unrighteousness' (*2 Ts 2:10–12*). In fact, when he (the Antichrist) will come, resolved to consummate all apostasy and finish his work, he will sit in the temple of God and be worshipped as Christ by those he has deceived (*2 Ts 2:4*). Rightly then shall he be cast into the lake of fire (*Ap 19:20*), and at the proper time God, in his own prescience, seeing all things when the right time come will send such a man, 'that they should believe a lie: that they all might be damned who believed not the truth, but had pleasure in unrighteousness' (*2 Ts 2:11–12*).

Contra Heresies (Adversus Haereses), V, xxv; L, xxviii, 1–2

Tertullian, Quintus Septimus Florens (Carthage 155–230)

Tertullian practised law in Rome before conversion and returning to Carthage. He is credited with the invention of theological Latin and importing the terminology of Roman law into theological dispute. The first of Cacciari's passages is drawn from his treatise on the 'Resurrection of the Flesh', *which complemented the polemical* 'On the Flesh of Christ' *in arguing against gnostic positions regarding the incarnation and the resurrection. The second is from the Apology addressed to Roman provincial governors arguing that Christians are good citizens in spite of their reluctance to sacrifice to the Emperor, the first of a line of political-theological reflections that would culminate in Augustine's* City of God *(tr.).*

XXIV–XXV. What these times are, you may come to learn along with the Thessalonians. As we read: 'how ye turned to God from idols to serve the living and true God; and to wait for his Son from heaven, Jesus, whom he raised from the dead' (*1 Ts 1:9–10*). And elsewhere: 'For what is our hope, or joy, or crown of rejoicing? Are not even ye in the presence of our Lord Jesus Christ at his coming?' (*1 Ts 2:19*). Similarly, 'before God, even our Father, at the coming of our Lord Jesus Christ with all his saints' (*1 Ts 3:13*). He instructs them that they should not have sorrow for the dead, he also explains to them the time of the resurrection: 'For if we believe that Jesus died and rose again, even so they also which sleep in Jesus will God bring with him. For this we say unto you by the word of the Lord, that we who are alive *and* remain unto the coming of the Lord shall not prevent them who are asleep. For the Lord himself shall descend from heaven with a shout, with the voice of the archangel, and with the trump of God: and the dead in Christ shall rise first: then we who are alive *and* remain shall be caught up together with them in the clouds, to meet the Lord in the air: and so shall we ever be with the Lord' (*1 Ts 4:14–17*). What archangel's voice, what trumpet of God is heard save in the halls of the heretics? Even if it were possible to receive the word of the Gospel that is like the trump of God calling out to men, they either are already dead in body, in a way that they can arise from the dead (but in this case how could they be alive?), or they are caught up in the clouds (but then how could they have ever been here?). As the apostle averred (*1 Cor 15:19*), those who only have hope in this life will be excluded from what is promised beyond it, even as they strive to grasp it with their hands, and will be deemed the most miserable of men; and, like Phigellus and Hermogenes, they deceive themselves regarding the truth (*2 Tm 1:15*). It is thus suggested in the *Second epistle to Thessalonians* that the divine authority of the Holy Ghost thoroughly grasps those thoughts: 'But of the times and the seasons, brethren, ye have no need that I write unto you. For yourselves know perfectly that the day of the Lord so cometh as a thief in the night. For when they shall say, Peace and safety; then sudden destruction cometh upon them, as travail upon a woman with child; and they shall not escape' (*1 Ts 5:1–3*). Furthermore, in the second epistle addressing the same people with even greater zeal, he says: 'Now we beseech you, brethren, by the coming of our Lord Jesus Christ, and *by* our gathering together unto him, that ye be not soon shaken in mind, or be troubled, neither by spirit, nor by word, nor by letter as from us, as that the day of Christ is at hand. Let no man deceive you by any means: for *that day shall not come*, except there come a falling away first, and that man of sin be revealed, the son of perdition; who opposeth and exalteth himself above all that is called God, or that is worshipped; so that he as God sitteth in the temple of God, shewing himself that he is God. Remember ye not, that, when I was yet with you, I told you these things? And now ye know what withholdeth that he might be revealed in his time. For the mystery of iniquity doth already work: only he who now letteth *will let*, until he be taken out of the way. And then shall that Wicked be revealed, whom the Lord shall consume with the spirit of his mouth, and shall destroy with the brightness of his coming: *even him*, whose coming is after the working of Satan with all power and signs and lying wonders, and with all deceivableness of unrighteousness in them that perish; because they received not the love of the truth, that they might be saved' (*2 Ts 2: 1–10*).

In John's *Revelation* where the succession of time unravels, the souls of the martyrs learn to endure beneath the altar and cry out to be avenged and judged (*Ap 6:9–11*), in order to let the world drain the last drop of all its plagues out of the cups of the angels (*Ap 15:7*); to let that Harlot City suffer its dues at the hands of the ten kings (*Ap 17:12*); to let the beast Antichrist and his false prophet wage war on the Church (*Ap 19:19–20*). So that after Satan has been cast into the bottomless pit for a while, and the dispensation of the first resurrection is given to those who are seated under the thrones (*Ap 20:2–4*), and after the time Satan is consigned to the flames (*Ap 20:10*), the judgement of universal resurrection shall be pronounced (*Ap 20:12*) in accordance with the scriptures.

On the Resurrection of the Flesh
(De Resurrectione carnis), XXIV, 1–20; XXV, 1–2

XXX. For the safety of the emperors we offer our prayers to the eternal God, the true God, the living God, whose favour even emperors court above all other gods. They know well who gave them their power; and, being human, also know who gave them life; knowing that this is the only God on whose might they depend, they are second to Him and first after Him, before and above all other gods. How could it be otherwise, since they stand above all living men, who, being living, take precedence over the dead? To the extent they think on the value of their power in this world they come to understand God; they acknowledge that they owe their power to Him over Whom they have no power. Then can the emperor lay waste the heavens and drag them in triumph at his chariot? Can he post sentries in heaven? Impose taxes on heaven? He cannot. For he is great only because he is less than heaven, and he belongs unto Him to whom the heavens and all creatures belong. He owes his empire to Whom, being first human, he owes his life; his power and his breath have the same source. We Christians raise our eyes and lift our hands to heaven in all innocence, and keep our heads uncovered for we have no cause to be ashamed, nor do we need special instruction for we pray with our hearts, we pray for all emperors to have a long life, a peaceful reign, a safe house, powerful armies, a loyal senate, a virtuous people, a world without strife, and whatever a man or Caesar could desire.

XXXII. There is another even greater necessity to pray for the good of the Caesars, and indeed for the stability of the Roman dominion and the whole empire, for we are aware the

Roman Empire has deferred the immeasurable calamity looming over the whole world and threatens with terrible woes. We certainly don't wish for this eventuality and we pray that such an end is deferred longer still and hope for the empire's long duration. At the same time our oaths are not taken upon the guardian spirits (*genii*) of the Caesars, but only upon the latters' safety, which is of much greater value than any spirit could be. Could you be so ignorant of the fact that these spirits are called *daemones*, a diminutive of *Daemon*? With regard to Caesars then we respect what God ordained, for He made them head over the rest; we see God's will in the Caesars and we can only desire the safety of that which God has willed. To us this is the greatest of pledges. On the other hand, it is our practice to ward off demons, that is spirits (*genii*), by expelling them from humanity. We do not take oaths by their name, nor do we show them the reverence due only to God.

The Apology (*Apologeticus Adversus Gentes pro Christianis*), *XXX, 1–4; XXXII, 1–3*

Hippolytus of Rome
(Asia 170–Sardinia 235)

Hippolytus of Rome was Presbyter in the Roman Church and author of a Refutation of all Heresies. Cacciari's texts are taken from his Commentary on the Book of Daniel and his Proof of Christ and the Antichrist (tr.).

XXI–XXII. Since the word of God is right but 'all men *are* liars' (*Ps 116:11*) as the scriptures say, let us examine if Paul's words accord with the Lord's. Writing to Thessalonians he urges them to be always alert and to continue praying without waiting for the Day of Judgement, because the fullness of time was not yet come, he puts it this way, 'Now we beseech you, brethren, by the coming of our Lord Jesus Christ, and *by* our gathering together unto him, That ye be not soon shaken in mind, or be troubled, neither by spirit, nor by word, nor by letter as from us, as that the day of Christ is at hand. Let no man deceive you by any means: for *that day shall not come*, except there come a falling away first, and that man of sin be revealed, the son of perdition; Who opposeth and exalteth himself above all that is called God, or that is worshipped; so that he as God sitteth in the temple of God, shewing himself that he is God. Remember ye not, that, when I was yet with you, I told you these things? And now ye know what withholdeth that he might be revealed in his time. For the mystery of iniquity doth already work: only he who now letteth *will let*, until he be taken out of the way. And then shall that Wicked be revealed, whom the Lord shall consume with the spirit of his mouth, and shall destroy with the brightness of his coming: *Even him*, whose coming is after the working of Satan with all power and signs and lying wonders' (*2 Ts 2:1–9*). Who is then that, up to the present, restrains (withholds) if not the fourth beast? The Deceiver shall come when this beast is removed and taken out of the way. But being excessively inquisitive on how many years are left before the beast is removed, means you don't realize you are starting the mischief of wishing to see the Day of Judgement come before its time. For it is said, 'Woe unto you that desire the day of the Lord!' and '*Shall* not the day of the Lord *be* darkness and not light?' (*Am 5:18–20*). Why then waste your time looking for that day when the Saviour himself has not revealed it? Tell me, do you know the day of your own death? Yet you want to deliberate over the end of the world! If God in his plentiful mercy was not patient with us, time would have come to an end long ago [...]. If God decrees the martyrs, who shed their blood for Christ, be patient then why can't you also wait, so that others can be saved and the number of the saints and the elect be complete?

XLIX–L. This was prophesied by Daniel on the subject of the Antichrist (*Daniel 11*): he shall be insolent, lusting for war, repressive and, after audaciously magnifying himself above every king and every god, boasting an army and sacking the walls of enemy cities, having power over treasures of gold and silver and precious stones, after speaking marvellous things against God, he shall want to be worshipped as God. All the Scriptures speak of him, and the prophets foretold of his coming and the ruin of the multitudes, the Lord bears them witness, and the apostles taught of the same things, and John in his Revelation spoke of him in mystic numbers. The Lord calls him 'abomination of desolation', while Paul says that he will show himself as the son of the Devil, 'after the working of Satan' (*2 Ts 2:9*). [...] He has raised himself above all kings and all gods, will rebuild the city of Jerusalem and erect anew the destroyed temple, will restore to the Jews all their lands and territories, and draw them from their slavery to the gentiles. He will proclaim himself their king. The infidels shall prostrate themselves before him as before God, thinking him to be the Christ, having not understood the words of the prophet, namely that he is a deceiver and a liar [. . .]. He shall kill the two witnesses and forerunners of Christ who preach his glorious *parousia* in Heaven. As the prophet says, 'I will give *power* unto my two witnesses, and they shall prophesy a thousand two hundred *and* threescore days, clothed in sackcloth' (*Ap 11:3*); similarly, the Angel said to Daniel: 'And he shall confirm the covenant with many for one week: and in the midst of the week he shall cause the sacrifice and the oblation to cease' (*Da 9:27*), we can understand this division of the week thus: the two witnesses and their announcement of the three and a half years time period represent the first half, the Antichrist, and his laying the world waste and waging war against the saints the second half, so that the prophecy be fulfilled: 'and the abomination that maketh desolate set up, *there shall be* a thousand two hundred and ninety days. Blessed *is* he that waiteth, and cometh to the thousand three hundred and five and thirty days' (*Da 12:11 ff.*).

LIII–LIV. And then, Daniel prophesies, two abominations, destruction and desolation. What could the former be if not the one wrought by Antiochus in his time[1] (*Da 11:21 ff.*)? And

---

[1] *Antiochus IV Epiphanes*, king of the Seleucid empire, attacked Jerusalem and put to death many of its inhabitants (167 BC).

what could the latter be if not the universal abomination wrought by the coming of the Antichrist? As Daniel says, 'he shall go forth with great fury to destroy, and utterly to make away many, and shall divide the land for gain, and he shall enter into the land, and shall overflow and pass over, and the land of Egypt shall not escape but these shall escape out of his hand, Edom, and Moab, and the chief of the children of Ammon' (*Da 11:36–45*); what is more, those with whom he shares the same blood will be the first to recognize him as king. These are, the Edomites, who descend from Essau and live on Mount Seir; then the Moabites and the Ammonites, descendants of Lot by his two daughters, as Isaiah says, 'But they shall fly upon the shoulders of the Philistines toward the west; they shall spoil them of the east together: they shall lay their hand upon Edom and Moab; and the children of Ammon shall obey them' (*Is 11:14*). The Antichrist, their proclaimed and glorified king, having overpowered the world with the abomination of desolation, will prevail for one thousand two hundred and ninety days as Daniel says: 'blessed *is* he that waiteth, and cometh to the thousand three hundred and five and thirty days' (*Da 12:12*); then, with the coming of dissolution and the persecution of the saints, whoever outlasts that day and near the forty-fifth day, while another Pentecost is looming, will inherit the kingdom of Heaven, as the Antichrist comes in the middle of fifty days; whereas the saints will rightly inherit the kingdom along with Christ.

LVI. Then, who could the two men on the opposite riverbanks be (*Da 12:5*) other than the Law and the prophets, and who was above the waters if not the very one about whom they once prophesied? Who was he, the man clothed in colourful linen with a writer's inkhorn at his side, if not the same one of whom, at the river Jordan at a later time, the Father will bear witness, and John will present to the people (*Ez 9:2*)? They [the Jews], therefore, who questioned him, knowing that all empires and all powers are his, came to see clearly that the world will be judged at the time all those wonders of which he spoke will be fulfilled. He, wanting to be believed, held up his right hand and his left hand to heaven, swearing by Him who lives forever (*Da 12:7*). Who is the one by whom Christ swore? It is evident that the Son is swearing by the Father; the Father lives for ever and not in time. And thus he swears: '*it shall be* for a time, times, and half *a time;* and – all these things will be known, when the world shall be finished' (ibid.). Then he outstretched his arms as a sign of patience. In saying, 'for a time, times, and half *a time*', he meant the three and a half years of the Antichrist: a time is a year, times are two years, and the half a time is half a year. Those are the one thousand two hundred and ninety days prophesied by Daniel.

Commentary on Daniel (Commentarius in Danielem),
XXI–XXII, XLIX–L, LIII–IV, LVI

V–VI. But the moment has come to broach the matter we have been anticipating, having said enough on the subject of the glory of God in the introduction, and it is proper that we look to the Holy Scriptures to find out what the coming of the Antichrist shall be; when, that is, in what age, in what time shall his iniquity be revealed, and whence and from what people shall he come, or what his name shall be – the Holy Scripture gives only a number; in what manner he shall lead people into error, gathering them from the ends of the earth; how he shall wear out and and persecute the saints; in what way he will be exalted as God; what his downfall will be that will reveal the Lord of Heaven; finally, what the conflagration of the entire world will be and what the glorious celestial kingdom of the saints, reigning with Christ, and what the eternal punishment by fire forced on the wicked shall be.

Like our Lord and God Jesus Christ, on account of his royalty and glory, was compared to a lion, so too and in a similar manner the Scriptures compare the Antichrist to a lion, on account of his tyranny and violence. For the deceiver wants to be like the Son of God in all things. So that if Christ is a lion, the Antichrist is also a lion, if Christ a king, then the Antichrist also a king. The Saviour is represented as a lamb, the Antichrist assumes the appearance of a lamb, even if a wolf inside. The Saviour came into the world in circumcision, the Antichrist will do the same. The Lord sent the apostles among the nations and the Antichrist will send his false apostles everywhere. As the Saviour gathered the scattered sheep so will the Antichrist gather the scattered people of the Jews. The Lord gave the seal[2] to his faithful,

---

[2] The seal of God, with which Christ stamps the foreheads of the faithful. The idea is that the stamp lets what is in Christ's mind be in the faithful (see *Cor 2:12*, and *2:16*), for that reason it has also been equated with the Holy Ghost. Paul uses the terms 'spirit of God' and 'Christ's mind' interchangeably (tr. note).

the Antichrist likewise. The Saviour assumed human form
and the Antichrist will too. The Saviour made a temple of his
flesh; in a similar manner the Antichrist will erect a temple of
stone in Jerusalem.

XV. It is from the tree of Dan that a tyrant and king will be
born and bred, wicked judge and son of the devil, as the
prophet testifies, 'Dan shall judge his people, as one of the
tribes of Israel' (*Gn 49:16*). One could say, however, that the
above referred to Sampson, who came from the line of Dan,
and was judge for twenty years. But the prophecy is partially
fulfilled in Sampson, whereas it will find its complete
fulfilment in the Antichrist. Jeremiah too speaks of this: 'The
snorting of his horses was heard from Dan: the whole land
trembled at the sound of the neighing of his strong ones' (*Jer
8:16*). And another prophet testifies: 'He shall gather together
all his forces from sunrise to sunset. And all shall follow him,
those he has summoned and those he has not. He shall turn
the sea white with the sails of his ships and the land dark with
his spears and shields. And every one meeting him in battle
shall fall to his sword'. All this is said of none other but the
insolent tyrant who is at war with God.

LXIII–LXIV. The blessed apostle Paul, writing to
Thessalonians, says, 'Now we beseech you, brethren, by the
coming of our Lord Jesus Christ, and *by* our gathering
together unto him, that ye be not soon shaken in mind, or be
troubled, neither by spirit, nor by word, nor by letter as from
us, as that the day of Christ is at hand. Let no man deceive you
by any means: for *that day shall not come*, except there come a

falling away first, and that man of sin be revealed, the son of perdition; who opposeth and exalteth himself above all that is called God, or that is worshipped; so that he as God sitteth in the temple of God, shewing himself that he is God. Remember ye not, that, when I was yet with you, I told you these things? And now ye know what withholdeth that he might be revealed in his time. For the mystery of iniquity doth already work: only he who now letteth *will let*, until he be taken out of the way. And then shall that Wicked be revealed, whom the Lord shall consume with the spirit of his mouth, and shall destroy with the brightness of his coming: *even him*, whose coming is after the working of Satan with all power and signs and lying wonders, and with all deceivableness of unrighteousness in them that perish; because they received not the love of the truth, that they might be saved. And for this cause God shall send them strong delusion, that they should believe a lie' (*2 Ts 2:1-11*). And also Isaiah, 'Let the wicked be cut off that he behold not the glory of the Lord'. Then, my beloved, once those things come to pass and the one week shall be rendered in two, the abomination of desolation shall rise, and the two prophets and the forerunner of the Lord having run their course and the whole world reaching its end, what shall remain but the coming from heaven of our Lord and Saviour Jesus Christ, Son of God, to whom we turn in hope? He shall bring universal conflagration and right judgement on all those who did not have faith in Him. He says, 'And when these things begin to come to pass, then look up, and lift up your heads; for your redemption draweth nigh' (*Lk 21:28*); 'But there shall not an hair of your head perish' (*Lk 21:18*); 'For as the lightning cometh out of the east, and shineth even unto the west; so shall also the coming of the Son of man be. For wheresoever the carcase is, there will the eagles be gathered together' (*Mt 24:27–28*). For there was a carcase in paradise too, there, cozened, Adam fell. Furthermore he says, 'the Son of Man shall send his angels and gather together his elect from the four winds of heaven' (*Mt 24:31*). But also David foretold the *parousia* (manifestation) of the Lord and his Judgement: 'His going forth *is* from the end of the heaven, and his circuit unto the ends of it and there is nothing hid from the heat thereof' (*Ps 19:6*). By the heat he means the conflagration. Not accidentally Isaiah says, 'Come, my people, enter thou into thy chambers, and shut thy doors about thee: hide thyself as it were for a little moment, until the indignation be overpast' (*Is 26:20*). And in like manner Paul, 'For the wrath of God is revealed from heaven against all ungodliness and unrighteousness of men, who hold the truth in unrighteousness' (*Rm 1:18*).

> *Demonstratio de Christo et Antichristo,*
> *V–VI, XV, LXIII–LXIV*

Origen (Alexandria 185–Tyre 254)

Origen was a prolific interpreter and theologian active in Alexandria and Caesaria. Cacciari's passage is drawn from his polemic with the neo-platonic philosopher Celsus claiming the superiority of Christianity to philosophy as a form of life and source of salvation (tr.).

Moreover, Paul in the second letter to Thessalonians shows in what manner there will be revealed 'the man of sin (*anomia*), the son of perdition (*apoleia*); who opposeth and exalteth himself above all that is called God, or that is worshipped; so that he as God sitteth in the temple of God, shewing himself that he is God' (*2 Ts 2:3–4*). And once again he says to the Thessalonians: 'And now ye know what withholdeth that he might be revealed in his time. For the mystery of iniquity doth already work: only he who now letteth *will let*, until he be taken out of the way. And then shall that Wicked be revealed, whom the Lord shall consume with the spirit of his mouth, and shall destroy with the brightness of his coming: *even him*, whose coming is after the working of Satan with all power and signs and lying wonders, and with all deceivableness of unrighteousness in them that perish; because they received not the love of the truth, that they might be saved' (*2 Ts 2:6–10*). And, expounding on the reason why the Wicked are allowed to live on, he explicitly said: 'because they received not the love of the truth, that they might be saved. And for this cause God shall send them strong delusion, that they should believe a lie: that they all might be damned who believed not the truth, but had pleasure in unrighteousness' (*2 Ts 2:10–12*). Then let anyone say if any passage in the Gospel or in the epistles of the Apostle leaves room for suspecting these statements as predictions of 'sorcery'. Those who wish may further glean the prophecy regarding the Antichrist from *Daniel*. But Celsus falsifies the word of Jesus, since Jesus never said that there will be others who, like him, will work miracles, others who are wicked and sorcerers, yet Celsus claims that He said those words. The magic spells of Egypt were not like the divine grace of Moses, and in the end it was obvious that the spells of the Egyptians were the result of sorcery whereas those of Moses came truly from a divine power, similarly the works of the Antichrist, and of those who feign to work miracles pretending to be the disciples of Christ, are identified as wonders and false signs, for deceiving iniquity is irresistible to those who march to their ruin, while the work of Christ and his disciples had for their fruit not deception but the salvation of the soul. Who then could rationally argue that the greatest form of life, one that daily strives to mitigate the work of iniquity, could be born of deception?

Contra Celsus, II, 50

Melito of Sardis (died Sardis c. 180–190)

Melito was Bishop of Sardis, and few of his works have survived. The passage in the Anthology chosen by Cacciari is a fragment surviving from his Apology for Christianity addressed to Marcus Aurelius, Emperor of Rome (tr.).

It has never come to pass before that the whole race of pious men will suffer such persecution perpetrated by the new decrees on all Asia. Shameless informers and those covetous of the riches of others, emboldened by those decrees, openly plunder and trample on innocent men, day and night.

If all that is what you (Marcus Aurelius) decreed then well and good. For it is not possible that a just prince could order something that is unjust; and we will gladly suffer the honour of such death. We only have this request: that you examine first those who have been ruined because of their tenaciousness by your decree, and then decide, on the grounds of your native fairness, whether any among them deserve to be put to torture and death, or live safe and secure. But if such a decision and such a decree, unprecedented even against enemy barbarians and not considered fit for them, if it not be proclaimed by you, then we beseech you even more, don't allow a similar public despoiling to continue to oppress us.

For our philosophy first took hold among the barbarians, but after flourishing among the nations, at the time of the great reign of Augustus, your ancestor, it became a blessing to the destiny of Rome.

Furthermore, from that time the majesty of the Roman Empire due to great conquests has grown; to this empire you are the designated successor, and so shall continue with your son, if now you provide protection for that philosophy that grew together with the empire, beginning with Augustus, that doctrine honoured by your ancestors along with other religions.

That our religion has flourished for the good of an empire with an auspicious beginning, can be proved by the fact that no calamity befell the dominions of Augustus, and, on the contrary everything has progressed favourably and prosperously in accordance with the wisdom and loyalty of all. Nero and Domitian alone, persuaded by some vile counsel, sought to accuse our religion. From then on slander against us has persisted and it is common practice to give credence to mindless chatter. Your pious fathers corrected their wrongs, frequently reprimanding in writing those who attempted to bring new measures against our religion. Among the most pious of your family your grandfather Hadrian, who sent letters to Minutius Fontanus, Proconsul of Asia, and many others. And your father too, at the time Hadrian ruled, wrote to the cities to prevent rioting against us, more specifically he wrote to the Larissaeans, the Thessalonians, the Athenians and to all the Greeks. Hence, we trust that you too may be disposed towards us in the same way as your ancestors; indeed, given that you are much more benevolent and learned, we trust that you will grant our request.

Fragments from Melito's Apology, in Eusebius of Cesarea, Ecclesiastical History (Fragmenta ex Apologia Melitonis, in Eusebius' Historia Ecclesiastica) IV, 26:5–11

Victorinus of Pettau (250–304)

Bishop of Poetovio in what was the Roman province of Panonia (located over the territory of parts of present day Hungary, Austria, Slovenia, Slovakia, Croatia, Serbia and Bosnia-Herzegovina) and author of biblical commentaries. Cacciari's selection is taken from his only surviving commentary on the Book of Revelation (tr.).

That the Antichrist should be numbered among the Caesars and those who lived in the great empire is expressly stated by Paul, for he says in his epistle to Thessalonians. 'And now ye know what withholdeth that he might be revealed in his time. For the mystery of iniquity doth already work: only he who now letteth *will let*, until he be taken out of the way. And then shall that Wicked be revealed, whom the Lord shall consume with the spirit of his mouth, and shall destroy with the brightness of his coming: *even him*, whose coming is after the working of Satan with all power and signs and lying wonders' (*2 Ts 2:6–9*). So that they knew he, who was then reigning supreme, would come, Paul added, 'the mystery of iniquity doth already work' (*2 Ts 2:7*), namely he speaks of the iniquity that he will effect in secret, but his power does not come from him or his father but is commanded by God. It is for this that Paul says: 'because they received not the love of the truth, that they might be saved ... for this cause God shall send them strong delusion, that they should believe a lie' (*2 Ts 2:10–11*). And Isaiah also says, 'they wait for light, but behold obscurity; for brightness, *but* they walk in darkness' (*Is 59:9*). And the Book of Revelation states that the prophets will be killed by him (i.e., the Antichrist) and on the fourth day will rise again, so that there be no one equal to God. Moreover, Jerusalem is called 'Sodom and Egypt' (*Ap 11:8*) and 'Sodom and Gomorra' in Isaiah (*Is 1:10*), on account of the evil-doing of the persecuting people. Therefore you need to follow the prophetic revelation with great care and attention to understand it, for the Holy Ghost speaks in perplexing ways, anticipating the

order of events running to the end of time, and back again to
the first time: revealing an event that will happen only once as
if it happened more than once.

Scholiums on the Book of Revelation
(Scolia in Apocalypsin), XI, 4–5

Ambrosiaster

Ambrosiaster is the author of a group of commentaries on Paul
previously attributed to St Ambrose, Bishop of Milan. The little
that is known of Ambrosiaster establishes him in Rome in 366–388
AD *as a member of the Roman clergy. Cacciari's selection is taken*
from the commentary on 2 Thessalonians Chapter 2 (tr.).

'Remember ye not, that, when I was yet with you, I told you
these things? And now ye know what withholdeth that he
might be revealed in his time' (*2 Ts 2:5–6*) – Paul said, 'what
withholdeth' will last as long as he who shall come before the
Lord is not revealed, and as a consequence, until the hope for
the coming of the Lord is fulfilled. This sequence of events is
earlier stated, in confidence, thus, 'for *that day shall not come*,
except there come a falling away first' (*2 Ts 2:3*) – I mentioned
before that this 'falling away' (*apostasia/defectio*) must be
understood as the fall of the Roman Empire: in fact, when
there will be *rebellion* the Antichrist will come, and only then
can we hope that the coming of the Lord is nigh.

For the mystery of iniquity doth already work: 'only he
who now letteth *will let*, until he be taken out of the way'

(*2 Ts 2:7*). The mystery of iniquity began with Nero, who had the apostles put to death for worshipping idols – since his father, the Devil, egged him on to do it – then continued with Diocletian and more recently with Julian, who could not bring persecution to its successful conclusion, for despite the fact that he started it with craft and skill, Heaven did not allow it. Well, Satan uses these agents, on the one hand, to mock the manifestation of the one true God, and, on the other, to entice men to worship many gods, as long as the Roman Empire lasts – or as Paul says, 'until he be taken out of the way'.

Commentary on Paul's Second Epistle to Thessalonians
(*In epistulam Beati Pauli ad Thessalonicenses secundam*)

John Chrysostom (Antioch 344/54– Pontic Comana 407)

John Chrysostom was Bishop of Constantinople and a prominent early Church Father, renowned for his eloquence and his commitment to ecclesiastical reform. His preaching consisted largely of biblical exegesis and commentary. The present passage has been taken from his commentary on Thessalonians (tr.).

[And now ye know what withholdeth that he might be revealed in his time. For the mystery of iniquity doth already work: only he who now letteth *will let*, until he be taken out of the way. And then shall that Wicked be revealed, whom the Lord shall consume with the spirit of his mouth, and shall destroy with the brightness of his coming: *even him*, whose coming is after the working of Satan with all power and signs and lying wonders (*2 Ts 2:6–9*).] One may rightly first ask, what is that which withholds, and then may want to understand the reason Paul speaks so equivocally of it. What then is this that 'withholdeth that he might be revealed'? That stops him [the Messiah] from being revealed? Some claim that it is the 'grace of the Holy Spirit'; others maintain, instead, that it is the Roman Empire. I'm in full agreement with the latter. For what reason? Because if Paul meant to understand it as the Holy Spirit he would not have spoken obscurely, he would have plainly said that even now the grace of the Holy Spirit, i.e., all charisma and gifts, withholds him. Otherwise, if he were about to come, for if he were to come when all grace and gifts lost most their power, he ought to have already come, since by now all those have lost all their power. But if instead Paul understands what withholds as the Roman Empire he has cause to be cryptic and enigmatic: for he did not want to attract unnecessary hostilities and futile dangers. Had he said that the Roman Empire was about to be overthrown, he knew he would have been accused of being evil and destructive, and with him all the faithful who live and strive under his guiding figure. For this reason he did not say, neither in this way nor in any direct way, what would come to pass, although he means to say the same thing. What thing? That the mystery of iniquity may be revealed in its own time, even if it is already at work. He says that Nero is some form of Antichrist – he wanted to be regarded as a god. Understandably then Paul speaks of a 'mystery', for he will not speak openly and shamelessly as Nero did. If before that time there was one – Paul says – who was not all that different from the Antichrist in wickedness, then what is strange about his imminent coming? And the reason the Apostle did not speak plainly was not that he was unclear about the matter, was not because of cowardice but rather to warn us not to attract unnecessary hostility, for nothing calls for impatience. But he also said, 'only he who now letteth *will let*, until he be taken out of the way' [i.e., the one who up to now withholdeth'], and this should be understood that as soon as the Roman Empire is finally 'taken out of the way' the Antichrist shall come. And naturally. For as long as the fear of such power lasts, no one will easily submit, but as soon as this empire disintegrates and falls into anarchy, the power of men and God will be attacked. In this way all the kingdoms that preceded this one were destroyed, for example, the kingdom of the Medes by the Babylonians, the kingdom of the Babylonians by the Persians, their kingdom by the Macedonians, the Macedonians by the Romans, so too this kingdom [of which the Apostle speaks] will be destroyed by the Antichrist and he will be destroyed by Christ, and the Antichrist will no longer last. Daniel too speaks of all these things with great clarity. Paul says, 'And then shall that Wicked be revealed'. What then? It is quite a consolation that he adds, 'the Lord shall consume [the Wicked] with the spirit of his mouth, and [he] shall destroy with the brightness of his coming (*parousia*) . . . the working of Satan with all power'. As a rapidly spreading fire attacking the young of little animals that first stuns and then consumes them, so the Will and

Coming (*parousia*) of Christ will take the Antichrist out of the way. Before the presence of Christ these things will disintegrate and even his mere appearance will suffice to halt all the work of deceit. Furthermore, [the apostle wished to point out] who is the one 'whose coming is after the working of Satan with all power and signs and lying wonders'. That is, that Antichrist will show all his power for signs and wonders but nothing will be true and all will be at the service of deceit. [Paul said] those things so that [the Christians] of the time would not be misled. And, he emphasizes, 'lying wonders', that is deceit and all that tempts us to unrighteousness. 'And with all deceivableness of unrighteousness in them that perish' (*2 Ts 2:9–10*). Why then, you may ask, God allowed him to be, and what kind of divine dispensation is this? What is to be gained by the coming of that Antichrist, since it bodes nothing but evil abuse for us? Fear not, beloved, and only harken him who says: he [the Antichrist] has power over those who will perish, all those who, were not the Antichrist come, would still have no faith. You ask again, what is to be gained in his coming? That those who perish will have their mouths sewn fast. How so? Because they will not believe in Christ, whether he is come or not. Therefore, he [the Antichrist] comes to control (manipulate) them, so that they are not able to say: 'we did not believe in Christ, not because Christ said he is God – even though He nowhere openly said that – but because they who came after Him preached it. Because we heard that there is only one God, the Creator of all things, and that is the reason we did not believe in Christ'. The Antichrist, therefore, is come to remove this pretext of theirs. For when the Antichrist is come and they believe in him, although he brings not righteousness but iniquity, then their mouths will be truly shut. For if you don't believe in Christ you have even greater cause not to believe in the Antichrist. For Christ said he was sent in the name of the Father, whereas the Antichrist said the opposite. And so Christ says: 'I am come in my Father's name, and ye receive me not: if another shall come in his own name, him ye will receive' (*John 5:43*). Still they will insist, 'but we have seen signs and wonders', but Christ also showed them great marvels. Thus they had greater reason to have faith in Christ than the Antichrist. Besides, many a thing has been prophesied about the Antichrist, that he is Wicked (*anomos*), that he is the Son of Perdition, and his coming is the work of Satan, whereas about Christ the opposite has been said, that he is the Saviour, and he brings boundless blessings, 'And for this cause God shall send them strong delusion, that they should believe a lie: that they all might be damned who believed not the truth, but had pleasure in unrighteousness' (*2 Ts 2:11–12*).

Commentary on the Second Epistle to
Thessalonians, Homily, IV

Augustine of Hippo (Thagaste, Roman Africa 354–Hippo 430)

Augustine was a major Latin theologian and Bishop of Hippo. Author of the justly famed Confessions *and the most influential apology for Christianity and statement of its political theology,* City of God. *He participated in many theological polemics and was the author of biblical commentary and an influential meditation on the Trinity. The following passage is taken from Book XX of the* City of God *dedicated to the Last Judgement and the question of Law (tr.).*

I see that I must omit many of the statements of the gospels and epistles about this last judgement, that this volume may not become unduly long; but I can on no account omit what the Apostle Paul says, in writing to the Thessalonians, 'We beseech you, brethren, by the coming of our Lord Jesus Christ, . . .' (*2 Ts 2:1–12*).

No one can doubt that he wrote this of the Antichrist and of the Day of Judgement, which he here calls the day of the Lord, nor that he declared that this day should not come unless he first came who is called the apostate – apostate, to wit, from the Lord God. And if this may justly be said of all the ungodly, how much more of him? But it is uncertain in what temple he shall sit, whether in that ruin of the temple which was built by Solomon, or in the Church; for the apostle would not call the temple of any idol or demon the temple of God. And on this account some think that in this passage Antichrist means not the prince himself alone, but his whole body, that is, the mass of men who adhere to him, along with him their prince; and they also think that we should render the Greek more exactly were we to read, not in the temple of God, but for or as the temple of God, as if he himself were the temple of God, the Church. Then as for the words, And now ye know what withholds, i.e., you know what hindrance or cause of delay there is, that he might be revealed in his own time; they show that he was unwilling to make an explicit statement, because he said that they knew. And thus we who have not their knowledge wish and are not able even with pains to understand what the apostle referred to, especially as his meaning is made still more obscure by what he adds. For what does he mean by 'For the mystery of iniquity does already work: only he who now holds, let him hold until he be taken out of the way: and then shall the wicked be revealed'? I frankly confess I do not know what he means. I will nevertheless mention such conjectures as I have heard or read.

Some think that the Apostle Paul referred to the Roman Empire, and that he was unwilling to use language more explicit, lest he should incur the calumnious charge of wishing ill to the empire which it was hoped would be eternal; so that in saying, For the mystery of iniquity does already work, he alluded to Nero, whose deeds already seemed to be as the deeds of Antichrist. And hence some suppose that he shall rise again and be Antichrist. Others, again, suppose that he is not even dead, but that he was concealed that he might be supposed to have been killed, and that he now lives in concealment in the vigour of that same age which he had reached when he was believed to have perished, and will live until he is revealed in his own time and restored to his kingdom. But I wonder that men can be so audacious in their conjectures. However, it is not absurd to believe that these words of the apostle, Only he who now holds, let him hold until he be taken out of the way, refer to the Roman Empire, as if it were said, Only he who now reigns, let him reign until he be taken out of the way. And then shall the wicked be revealed: no one doubts that this means Antichrist. But others think that the words, You know what withholds, and The mystery of iniquity works, refer only to the wicked and the hypocrites who are in the Church, until they reach a number so great as to furnish the Antichrist with a great people, and that this is the mystery of iniquity, because it seems hidden; also that the apostle is exhorting the faithful tenaciously to hold the faith they hold when he says, Only he who now holds, let him hold until he be taken out of the way, that is, until the mystery of iniquity which now is hidden departs from the Church. For they suppose that it is to this same mystery John alludes when in his epistle he says, 'Little children, it is the last time: and as you have heard that Antichrist shall come, even now are there many antichrists; whereby we know that it is the last time. They went out from us, but they were not of us; for if they had been of us, they would no doubt have continued with us' (*1 John 2:18–19*). As therefore there went out from the Church many heretics, whom John calls many antichrists, at that time prior to the end, and which John calls the last time (*novissima*), so in the end they shall go out who do not belong to Christ, but to that last (*novissimum*) Antichrist, and then he shall be revealed.

City of God XX, 19:1–3

Theodoret of Cyrrhus (Antioch 393– Cyrrhus 458)

Theodoret was Bishop of Cyrrhus, remembered for his controversial positions on the trinity and in particular on the humanity of Christ. He as also the author of biblical exegesis, an apology for Christianity and a Compendium of Heretical Fables. *Cacciari draws his selections from the commentary on Thessalonians and the* Compendium *(tr.).*

Some interpreters have taken 'what withholdeth' (*2 Ts 2:6*) to be referring to the Roman Empire, while others to the Holy Spirit. But, as he would say, if it were the Holy Spirit that opposes and withholds, it [the *katechon*] would not have transpired. Further, it is not possible that the Holy Spirit is wholly consumed. In what way could those who are beyond spiritual succour ever overpower its plan? Similarly, the Roman Empire will not be followed by another. It is not by chance that the divine Daniel represents the Roman Empire as the fourth beast, a beast with a little horn on its head with which it makes war against the saints. The creature of this prophecy is also found in what the divine Apostle said. But I think he did not mean either of the above two things, and I myself believe what others have said on the matter to be more accurate. For the God of all things has decreed that he [the Antichrist] be revealed at the precise time of the End. Therefore, it is God's will that withholds him and prevents his manifestation. For this reason, I think the above verses have another meaning. More clearly, God instructed the divine Apostle on the necessity of proclaiming the Gospel unto the nations and it is only then that the End will come to pass; observing the prevalence of idolatry, and following the Lord's tenets, he stated that the forces of superstition must be first dispersed and only then, once the divine gospel burns bright, shall the Adversary of truth be revealed.

[*2 Ts 2:7.*] 'For the mystery of iniquity doth already work'. – Some have said that the 'mystery of iniquity' refers to Nero, and have further added that he was the architect of ungodliness. I, on the other hand, believe that the Apostle in these verses refers to the heresies that were on the rise at the time. It is through heresy that the devil, having turned many away from the path of truth, prepares the way for destructive deceit. That is the reason [the Apostle] defined as the 'mystery of iniquity' those who have an occult link to iniquity. In fact, the devil flagrantly keeps humans away from God. It is for that reason the Apostle calls his coming a 'revelation', for shamelessly and tirelessly will he preach his schemes and machinations. 'He who now letteth *will let,* until he be taken out of the way'. That is, it is necessary the error of superstition come to an end and that the Gospel be proclaimed.

Commentary on the Second Epistle to Thessalonians
(Interpretatio in epistulam secundam ad Thessalonicenses)

Let us remember what the Apostle often taught them, he says: 'Remember ye not, that, when I was yet with you, I told you these things? And now ye know what withholdeth that he [the Antichrist] might be revealed in his time' (*2 Ts 2:5–6*). He says, he would have already come if God's grace would not have stopped him, by postponing his coming (*parousia*) until the proper time. 'For the mystery of iniquity doth already work' – by this verse he means to indicate the heresies on the rise at the time. 'Only he who now letteth *will let*, until he be taken out of the way' (*2 Ts 2:7*) – by this he means that God's decree will withhold his coming. It is necessary that, and in accordance with divine providence, the Gospel is proclaimed unto the nations, and only then the Antichrist will come.

Compendium of Heretical Accounts
(Haereticarum fabularum compendium), V, 23

Theodore the Interpreter (aka Theodore of Mopsuestia, or Theodore of Antioch) (Antioch 393–Mopsuestia 460)

Theodore was Bishop of Mopsuestia and friend of John Chrysostom and author of innovative biblical exegesis, including commentaries on Paul from which this extract has been taken (tr.).

2 Ts 2:6–8. It does not seem convincing to me that [what withholds refers to the blessings of the Holy Spirit]; for these blessings have already died out. Should then one say that these blessings are still being received because some people, from time to time, continue to pray, some [blessings] would not die even in such time, for the saints could not completely disappear. But even then there will be people who reject his doctrine and they will recognize themselves in the striving for mercy. Moreover, insofar as that which 'withholds' is concerned he says, that the nature of evil is to withhold, but God prevents him from doing it. So that the world will come to its End and he will then be revealed. Indeed, the Apostle states that a divine decision restrains the Iniquitous, and adds so 'that he might be revealed in his time'. As a matter of fact, the expression 'the mystery of iniquity doth already work', means to say that the devil does not work his apostasy openly but in secret, as he does with many things. Always marshalling his forces to try and throw the faithful out from the path of piety.

In epistulam posteriorem Pauli ad
Thessalonicenses Commentarii Fragmenta

Jerome (Stridon, Roman province of Dalmatia 342–Bethlehem 420)

Jerome was a pioneer of monastic asceticism, translator of the Bible into Latin (the Vulgate) and author of biblical exegesis and a wide-ranging correspondence. The present extract is drawn from the 121st letter, addressed to Algasius (tr.).

In those days the spirit of the Thessalonians was restless and disturbed, whether the reason be an ill-understood letter, or a false revelation that deceived them in their sleep, or the conjectures of some who had interpreted the words of Isaiah, Daniel and of the gospels on the Antichrist as referring to their time, they hoped that the coming of Christ in all his glory was imminent. The Apostle remedied this error, relating the events that must be awaited prior to the coming of the Antichrist, such that, when they had seen them, they would be able to recognize the advent of the Antichrist, that is the man of sin, the son of perdition, the Adversary, the one 'Who opposeth and exalteth himself above all that is called God, or that is worshipped; so that he as God sitteth in the temple of God'. He said that the *parousia* of the Lord would not happen without the *discessio,* in Greek the *apostasy*, such that all the peoples subject to the Roman Empire rebel, and it will be revealed, that is shown, just as all the prophets had proclaimed, the man of sin in whom is found the fount of all iniquity, the son of perdition, that is to say the son of the devil, for it is he who is the universal perdition – the adversary of Christ called for this reason the Antichrist, who will raise himself above every being called God, and will trample with his feet the gods of all the peoples just as with the revealed and true religion, and will sit in God's temple, whether this be in Jerusalem (as some think) or whether it is the Church (as we consider more likely) revealing himself as if he were Christ, the son of God. Christ will not come unless the Roman Empire is devastated and he is preceded by the Antichrist, for He is coming to destroy the Antichrist. Remember – he [Paul] says – what I have already spoken to you and what I am now writing in the letter, I say to you that Christ will not come unless he is preceded by the Antichrist, 'for that day shall not come, except there come a falling away first' – you know perfectly well what prevents the Antichrist from revealing himself immediately. He does not want to say directly the destruction of the Roman Empire, because its own leaders considered it eternal. For this reason, according to John's *Revelation*, the whore dressed in purple has the blasphemous name 'eternal Rome'. If the Apostle had said openly and defiantly: 'The Antichrist will not come before the destruction of the empire', it might have been sufficient cause for the persecution of the Church.

What follows, 'For the mystery of iniquity doth already work: only he who now letteth *will let*, until he be taken out of the way. And then shall that Wicked (*anomos*) be revealed' means this: the coming of the Antichrist is distributed across the numerous evils and sins with which Nero, the most impure of the Caesars, had oppressed the world. That which would be done later had already been partially accomplished by Nero – suffice only that the Roman Empire, that now holds within itself all the people, retreat (*recedat – recessio*) and remove itself. Then will come the Antichrist, source of iniquity, whom the Lord Jesus will destroy with the breath of his mouth, that is with his divine power and empire of his glory, 'where what he wills and commands is done (*cuius iussisse, fecisse est*),'[3] not in virtue of the strength of his soldiers and not with the aid of the angels. Immediately, all at once, as soon as he appears the Antichrist will be destroyed.

Epistle CXXI

---

[3] This line from Jerome is a reworking of verses 5–6 from *Psalms 148* (tr. note).

Cassiodorus, Flavius Marcus Aurelius, Senator (c. 485–c. 580)

Cassiodorus was a prominent figure in Roman political life who retired to a monastery in 540. He wrote on Roman law, Christian doctrine, a well-known text on the liberal arts as well as allegorical biblical exegesis. The following extract is drawn from his commentary on 2 Thessalonians (tr.).

2 Ts, 3 [Paul] appreciates the fact that the Thessalonians have seen correctly according to the rule of true faith; and he warns them that in future the perverse will deceive them with something entirely new and will say to them that the Lord will not come if the Antichrist has not shown himself first, and [Paul] describes his perverse times in a very detailed way. What is more, he says that the ministry of iniquity is already at work and warns too that the presence of absolute evil will necessarily manifest itself at the moment that the Roman Empire, which currently withholds, is removed and replaced by another order of things. That is to say, finally, that after these signs there will be the truth of the coming of God.

In epistulam secundam ad Thessalonicenses

Glossa Ordinaria

The Glossa Ordinaria *is a widely known medieval running commentary on the Bible compiled from many different sources.*

The present extract is taken from the commentary on the Second Thessalonians (tr.).

2 Ts 2:6, 'And now ye know what withholdeth that he might be revealed in his time'. The Apostle says that the Thessalonians know that which withholds, but do not openly say it, and thus we do not know whether it is that which some suspect; that it referred to the Roman Empire, in as much as it had not been removed. It is said that the Apostle did not wish to write it openly, in order not to risk calumny by wishing ill to the Roman Empire, since they hoped it would be eternal.

'In his time'. Once everyone had entered into the Roman Empire and obedience to the Church in Rome, the time of *discessio* would come between both empires; and once completed this *discessio* would become that of the iniquitous, that is when the time of mercy during which all the peoples adhered to the faith had been completed. Only then will the *discessio* manifest itself and thus will the day of the Lord be nigh.

2 Ts 2:7, 'For the mystery of iniquity doth already work: only he who now letteth *will let*, until he be taken out of the way'. Iniquity was there even at the very beginning of the faith, but as a mystery of iniquity masquerading as piety, which is to say that even though there were false priests they nevertheless wanted to be considered priests of Christ. The devil killed martyrs by means of Nero and others, and did so openly, killing Elijah and Enoch and many others. Nero and others were shadows of the future Antichrist, in the same way that David and Abel were shadows of Christ.

'Taken out of the way' [One should understand this to mean]: until the power of the Roman Empire is removed from the centre of the world. Indeed, all and from every part flowed into Rome as to the head. Or, in another way: those who possess faith will keep it until it is cooled. Or still further: he who withholds the Iniquitous, leading one to faith, withholds him as far as that faith is not taken out of the way. Or indeed: until the mystery of iniquity is removed from the centre, that is from among ordinary things, when men no longer are ashamed to be adulterers or thieves, just as they are not ashamed to walk or to talk.

'Out of the way' – It is certain that here we speak of the *discessio*, its open manifestation. Then, once revealed the *discessio* from the truth God, when all charity is frozen, the Antichrist will reveal himself in the abundance of iniquity.

Adso of Montier-en-Der, France (910/15–992)

Adso of Montier was Abbot of Montier-en-Der and a prominent and prolific writer in the tenth century (tr.).

It is because of the coming of that time in which the Antichrist will reveal himself, that is, when the Day of Judgement begins to dawn, that the Apostle Paul said in the *Letter to Thessalonians*: 'Now we beseech you, brethren, by the coming of our Lord Jesus Christ' (*2 Ts 2:1*). He further said in the same passage 'for that day shall not come, except there come a falling away (*apostasy*) first, and that man of sin be revealed (*apocalypse*), the son of perdition' (*2 Ts 2:3*). Indeed, we know very well that after the reign of the Greeks and after the reign of the Persians, when each of them in their time enjoyed great fame and acted with maximum power, and so on until the last empire, after all the other empires rose the empire of the Romans, which was the most powerful of all the great empires that ever existed and which had under its power all the other reigns of the earth and all the peoples who had submitted to the Romans and were 'subject to the tribute'. It is on the basis of this that the Apostle Paul says that the Antichrist will not come on earth 'except there come a falling away first' (*2 Ts 2:3*), and this means that the Antichrist will not come before all the reigns that were originally subject to the empire had distanced themselves from the Roman Empire. However, this time is still to come because although the Roman Empire has been largely destroyed as long as there remains, however, the King of the Franks, who maintain the Roman Empire and continue to govern, the power of the empire is not completely spent and is preserved in these kings. Indeed, our learned doctors say that it will be one of the kings of the Franks who will reconstruct the Roman Empire, who will appear in the last days, will be powerful and will be the last of the kings ever to exist. After having governed his kingdom happily, he will come at the end to Jerusalem where on the 'mount of olives' he will leave his sceptre and crown. This will be the end and the dissolution of the empire of the Romans and the Christians.

According to what the Apostle Paul has said in the letter, the Antichrist will come. And, speaking here of him, 'the man of iniquity' 'will reveal himself', and although he is a man, he will be the source of all evil and the 'son of perdition', that is to say 'the son of the devil', and that not so much by nature as more by imitation, he will be that from the moment when he will do nothing but accommodate himself to the will of the devil. 'For the fullness' of diabolic authority and complete knowledge of evil 'lives in him, in whom all the treasures' of malice and malignity 'will be hidden'. 'Who opposeth' means that the Antichrist is opposed to Christ and to all his followers – and 'exalteth' which means that 'exalteth himself above all that is called God, or that is worshipped', that is above all the Gods of the nations, Hercules, Apollo, Jove, Mercury who other pagans deem to be their Gods. The Antichrist raises himself above all these Gods from the moment he becomes greater and more powerful than they, but also above 'all those that are the objects of worship' which is to say above the Holy Trinity that is the only [God] that must necessarily remain adored and celebrated by every creature, 'so that he as God sitteth in the temple of God, shewing himself that he is God'. Indeed, as we said above, although born in the city of Babylon, he will be coming to Jerusalem, he will circumcise himself, and he will say to the Jews, 'I am the Christ' promised to you and who has come for your salvation, for he can 'bring together those who have been dispersed' and defend them. And so all the Jews will bow down before him, believing to accept God while accepting the Devil. Notably, it is also said that the 'Antichrist' 'resides in the Temple of God' which is to say the holy church, rendering all Christians martyrs and raising himself and glorifying himself since the Devil 'is a king over all the children of pride' (*Job 41:34*) and will show himself to be the origin of all evil.

Two honourable prophets shall be sent to the world before the coming of the Antichrist in order to ensure that he does not come immediately and without warning to deceive and definitively ruin the entire human race. Enoch and Elizah will teach and preach for three and a half years, arming the faithful with divine arms against the force of the Antichrist, comforting them and preparing the elect for war. What is more, these two noble prophets and teachers will convert all the sons of Israel, who will then find themselves in the grace of the faith, and will protect the faith, along with the elect, from the violence of such unbridled force. And so it will come to pass, as is written in the scripture: 'although the number of the children of Israel be as the sand of the sea, a remnant shall be saved' (*Rm 9:27*). Thus, when they have completed their three and a half years of preaching, the persecution of the Antichrist will be released immediately and he will unleash upon them his armies and will kill them, as it is said in the *Revelation*: 'And when they shall have finished their testimony, the beast that ascendeth out of the bottomless pit shall make war against them, and shall overcome them, and kill them' (*Rev 11:7*). Therefore, after these two are killed, the persecution of the remaining faithful will raise either martyrs or apostates. And all who believe in him will bear 'his sign on their foreheads'.

Since we have spoken of the beginnings of the Antichrist we must now speak of his end. The Antichrist or 'son of the devil' and the fearsome father of all evil, is predicted to afflict all the world with persecution and to torment God's people with many sufferings for three and a half years. Having killed Enoch and Elias and having crowned with martyrdom those who persevered in the faith, 'the judgement of God' will fall on the Antichrist, as Paul said 'destroying the Antichrist with the breath from his mouth'. Whether he is killed by the power of Christ's own strength or by the Archangel Michael, the Antichrist will fall by virtue of the strength of our Lord Jesus Christ and not that of an angel or archangel. Our teachers say that the Antichrist will be killed in his tent and on his throne on the Mount of Olives, at the same place where our Lord ascended to heaven. Furthermore, you must know that the Day of Judgement will not immediately follow the killing of the Antichrist but, as we know from the book of Daniel, God will concede forty days for those elect seduced by the Antichrist to 'perform penitence'. After this penitence no one can know how much time remains until 'the Lord comes in judgement' – all is in the hands of God who will judge the world that must be judged at an hour that was chosen by him centuries before.

Treatise on the Antichrist 97–195

Bruno the Carthusian (Cologne 1030– Serra San Bruno 1101)

Bruno was the founder of the Carthusian order. The text below is taken from his commentary on Second Thessalonians (tr.).

'And now ye know what withholdeth that he might be revealed in his time' (*2 Ts 2:6*). The Antichrist will come when the *apostasy* has been fulfilled – and you know very well what it is that withholds it and prevents it from happening. That is to say that it withholds so that the works of the Antichrist will be revealed in their time, that is to say at the right time. If instead he were to come while the unity of the faith and the Christian empire still held, then this would not be the right time for him to reveal himself. Truly, he will reveal himself in his own time; now the mystery of iniquity is at work and it is not his time – his is a time of a hidden and spiritual iniquity present in the members that precede their nefarious head. Only this is left for his revelation: he who holds him back, withholds his coming, in other words the Christian empire and the unity of the faith are taken out of the way, that is removed from the community. Like a dead man is removed from the community of living men.

Expositio in epistulam Pauli secundam
ad Thessalonicenses

Otto of Friesing (Klostenburg 1114–Morimond Abbey 1158)

Otto was Bishop of Friesing and a member of the Cistercian order who was active in the Second Crusade. He introduced the study of Aristotle to Germany and is remembered as a historian of The Deeds of Frederick Barbarossa. The present extracts are taken from his other major historical work The Two Cities, A Chronicle of Universal History to the Year 1146 AD *(tr.).*

So, when Nero sought to destroy the City of God by persecuting the Christians he crowned with blessed martyrdom two of the most blessed of the Apostles, Peter and Paul, commanding that Peter be hung on the cross feet uppermost and that Paul be executed by the sword. For this act the city of Rome would pay immense consequences in the following year, when it was devastated by a plague of such scale that there were over 30,000 funerals. Processo, Marziani and many others fell to the same persecution. Lino succeeded Peter in Rome, Euodio in Antioch. During the same days two settlements in Britain were conquered with a massacre of citizens and allies. And more, still at the same time, Roman soldiers lost several provinces in the East and were ignominiously submitted to the yoke of the Parthians. Three Asian cities: Laodicea, Hierapolis and Colosa were destroyed by an earthquake, and it should be noted that after the Apostles had been crowned with martyrdom the secular dignity of this city began to diminish.

No sooner had Nero learnt that Galba had been acclaimed Emperor in Spain by the army than, losing heart while interfering in public matters, he was declared a public enemy by the Roman Senate. And seeing that his corruption could not produce any effect, he fled four miles from the city and in the fourteenth year of his reign he killed himself. With him ended the family of the Caesars. There were those who said that what can be read in the Apostle ('and now you will know that which withholds his apocalypse, that will have its moment' and this is 'Whoever withholds, precisely until the means are taken away') was said with reference to Nero under whose reign Paul wrote. And further they thought Nero wasn't dead but removed alive from human affairs until the end-time when he would appear at the same age he had then, and that he would be the Antichrist.

> *Chronicles of the History of the Two Cities, III, 16:2–28*
> *(Chronica sive Hostira de duabus civitatibus)*

The City of Christ, as is taught in the Holy Scripture, suffered initially a violent persecution by the City of the World under tyrannical and unbelieving kings, then the fraudulent persecution of the heretics and then, thirdly, the deceptions of the hypocrites. And then there will come the last, as violent as it is fraudulent and deceptive, the worst of all, the one under the Antichrist. He opposes himself to Christ in everything, in life and in doctrine, even claiming to be Christ. He is called Antichrist because he is the opposite of Christ. In Greek they say *anti* for *contra*. Furthermore, it is believed that the Antichrist will come from the tribe of Dan, that is, from a servile condition, from that of which the Prophet said 'Dan is a snake on the road, is a worm on the path' (*Gen 49:17*).

What signs will precede the coming of the Antichrist are only hinted at by the Apostle when writing to the Thessalonians. He said, 'And now know who withholds his apocalypse will have his time. Already, in fact, the mystery of iniquity is abroad, but he who withholds, will withhold until, precisely, the means are removed'. And again, 'First must come the apostasy and the apocalypse of the man of *anomie*'. These things, as I have already mentioned, refer for some interpreters to Nero, under whose reign Paul was writing while for others, they refer to the devil, whose followers are all those who participate in the wicked city. These say that Paul meant Zebulun who worked the mystery of iniquity by persecuting the saints through his followers in the city. Zebulun worked *in his time*, that is to say at the end of time, because he manifested all the impiety and all the energy of impiety spread by means of the Antichrist. It can be read in the book of Revelation that after a thousand years, a number signifying the fullness of time, Satan who is now tied in the minds of the wicked, who hold within themselves wickedness as in an abyss, will be released, and will erupt in all his express iniquity, pouring forth in all his might. Note that Paul does not describe the wickedness of the present time as iniquity, but as *the mystery of iniquity*, thus all the sufferings undergone by the Church, from its beginning to the Antichrist, appear with respect to what will have to be undergone not as iniquity but as a mystery, that is to say as a figure of iniquity. Or it can be said: Paul calls *mystery* something hidden (we usually call secret things mystic) and this is the meaning: then the tribulations of the Church shall be manifest, dangerous and cruel when, in comparison with them, everything the Church has suffered or suffers could be put out of sight. And that which Paul says, continuing 'That which withholds will withhold until the means are removed' agrees with the meaning of the previous words: those who keep their vices hidden under earnest modesty until in the course of time these vices 'get in the way'; that is to say, the vices should not be publically revealed in their shameless face. Paul seems precisely to point to this by stating in advance, 'And now know that which withholds' until 'they are revealed in their time'. Indeed, it's as if he said that the Antichrist will not reveal himself until the time has come for the complete revelation of the wickedness of the Amorites (*Gen 15:16*). Then he says that even the revelation of the one who withholds will precede the final apostasy. Then truly the leader of error will show himself, when almost the whole world abandons truth and separates themselves from the author of truth. Some think this *separation* refers to the expression 'he who withholds will withhold, until he is removed' and attribute it to the kingdom (Roman Empire). They interpret it in this way: since all oppose themselves to justice, love sin and thus separate themselves from the justice of the kingdom, whoever reigns over the kingdom will fall into the misery of losing all respect and becoming a common man, like one who comes from the mass of the plebs. For they say the Apostle hid these things behind a mask and veil of words in order not to appear to insult the Roman Empire, considered eternal to those for whom he was writing. For when saying 'and now you will know who withholds' they understood him as saying that he wants others to know with clear proofs that which you know. But others interpret the meaning of these words as referring primarily to the kingdom, as if they referred to the priests and the seat of Rome.

> *Chronicle of the History of the Two Cities VIII, 1–2*
> (*Chronica sive Historia de duabus civitatibus*)

John Calvin (1509–1564)

Calvin was a leading French Reformer active in establishing theocratic rule in Geneva between 1541 and his death in 1564 and the inspiration of the international political theology of Calvinism. His major works were the 'Institutes of Christian Religion' and the 'Commentary on Romans'. The extract below is drawn from his commentary on Second Thessalonians (tr.).

2 Ts 2:6, 'That which withholds', means, in this case, precisely an impediment or a cause of delay. Chrysostom, who thinks that this expression can be understood only with reference to either the Spirit, or to the Roman Empire, inclines more to the second interpretation. And indeed for the plausible reason that if Paul had understood 'that which withholds' as the Spirit he would not have spoken in such enigmatic terms, but rather, intending by it the Roman Empire chose to avoid provoking hostility against his person. He offers also another reason for why the survival of the Roman Empire would delay the revelation of the Antichrist – just as the Babylonian monarchy was overcome by the Persians and the Medes and they in turn by the Macedonians, who in the end fell before the Romans, so it is evident that the

Antichrist would gather to himself the by now emptied hegemony of the Roman Empire. Nothing of what we have just said was not confirmed by subsequent events. Chrysostom indeed took account of historical reality. All the same, I am of the opinion that Paul intended something quite different, namely that the doctrine of the Gospel be spread throughout and to the point when nearly all of the world could be recognized as guilty of pride and obstinate wrong-doing. However, there can be no doubt that the Thessalonians had already heard from the mouth of Paul something about this 'impediment', whatever that was, from the moment the very same Paul recalled to their memory [the words they had earlier heard in his presence].

Let us, however, consider which of the two interpretations is the more probable: either Paul declared that the light of the gospels must necessarily be spread to all parts of the world before God would take the reigns from Satan, or that the power of the Roman Empire held back the rise of the Antichrist to the point that the latter could not erupt until the empire's power had been spent. For sure, it seems to me that Paul preached universally to the Gentiles – in fact God's grace must necessarily be offered to all – and that Christ passed through the whole of the world with his Gospel so that the impiety of men might be shown and condemned. Therefore, this delay would last until the journey of the Gospel had followed its course. And indeed, the exhortation of grace for salvation came first. At this point Paul uses the expression 'in its time' for when the moment of retribution arrived after grace had been refused.

2 Ts 2:7: The mystery of iniquity: this is opposed to revelation; since Satan has still not gathered sufficient force for the Antichrist openly to oppress the Church, Paul says that he is preparing in secret what he will be able to accomplish openly when his moment arrives. For the meantime he prepares in secret the foundations on which he will subsequently construct his edifice, as it happened. All this only goes to prove more convincingly my initial hypothesis that 'Antichrist' does not refer to an individual but to a kingdom that extends across several centuries. In the same way, John will say that the Antichrist is to come, but that there are also many antichrists already in his time (*John 1:2, 18*). He warns his contemporaries to try and defend themselves against this mortal peril that at that time raged and manifested itself in many guises. The sects spreading then were none other than the seeds of those infernal weeds that had wrapped around and almost destroyed the entire 'camp' of God. Although Paul supports the idea of a secret machination, he nevertheless uses the term 'mystery' and not any other expression, clearly meaning by this the 'mystery of salvation' of which he speaks often in other places (*Col 1:26*); indeed Paul consistently insists on the opposition between the Son of God and the 'son of perdition'.

Paul attributes the same subject to both expressions – indeed, the Antichrist will flourish for a fixed time and then will be summarily removed. I do not doubt that all this refers to the Antichrist and that the participle, *katechon*,[4] 'that which

---

[4] *katechon* is the participle of the verb *katechein*. See explanatory footnote XXX.

withholds', must be interpreted according to the future. For this reason, in my view, Paul added to console the believers that the reign of the Antichrist will be temporary, given that the time assigned to the Antichrist was fixed directly by God. To the objection of the believers that 'what is the point of preaching the Gospel if the tyranny of Satan threatens to last forever' Paul called for patience, for God will afflict his church for but a short period of time because it will, in the end, be liberated from the Antichrist. On the other hand, however, the eternity of the reign of Christ should not be forgotten so that believers can trust in this.

2 Ts 2:8: 'The impious will only be revealed in this way' which is to say not until 'that which withholds' will be completely removed. Paul is not referring to a time of revelation, when that which now holds supreme power will be 'removed' but to the time immediately preceding it. Indeed, Paul had just said that there was something that held back the Antichrist from being able to seize the kingdom openly. All the same, he also added that the Antichrist was preparing a secret plan of blasphemy. Finally Paul added the definitive consolation that in the end the tyranny of the Antichrist would come to its term. Now, he repeats once more, that whoever had until then remained hidden will be revealed 'in his time', and this repetition is perfectly coherent with the idea that the believers, being sustained by the arms of the Spirit, can effectively fight under the protection of Christ, avoiding defeat in this way even if blasphemy is able to disseminate itself even more rapidly.

Commentaries on the Letter of Paul to the Thessalonians

Appendix 2

Translator's Interview with Massimo Cacciari

EP: *To begin with, whence your interest in political theology and what is its place in your philosophical development?*

MC: I consider political theology to be an important aspect of European political philosophy. It is evident in ancient thought where there is a strong relation between the theological and the political dimension; suffice to recall that the Greeks used terms like *nomizein theos, nomiza tous theous* to say 'belief in God' and that *nomizein* has the same root as *nomos,* that is law. The link between the religious and political dimensions is constitutive of the ancient *polis* and would become fundamental for the Romans. When Cicero says that the Romans are the most religious people, what does he mean? He is referring to a link between the constitution of the Roman people, the political concept of the *populus* and the concept of *religio*, a typically Latin term for which there is no equivalent in other languages; Greek does not have any term equivalent to *religio* – it is an eminently Roman political term, for when one speaks of *religio* one means to say *religio civilis* or *religio populi romani*. It is impossible to avoid being interested in this link between theology and politics when working with Western European philosophy or with the politics and history of Western Europe.

EP: *Political theology has existed since the thought of Paul of Tarsus (*omnis potestas a Deo*) and is very present in medieval political philosophy from Augustine to Dante as well as in modern thought. Your book,* The Withholding Power *promises to make an original contribution to current English language debates in political theology which have been largely influenced by the work of Carl Schmitt and its reception. What is the contemporary relevance of political theology and what is your main difference with Schmitt?*

MC: The problem of political theology explicitly addressed in the philosophy of law and in twentieth-century political philosophy was shaped by Schmitt's studies and provocations. As is known, Schmitt maintained that political categories were formed through the secularization of elements drawn from the theological tradition. This particular understanding of political theology was obviously absent in the classical period, in Greece, Rome and the medieval times, which lacked the idea of secularization. In contemporary debates in the field of political theology the question of how the secularization of theological ideas into political concepts takes place is of particular importance. This theme is central to understanding major contemporary ideologies according to which many authors, not only Schmitt, read theological, that is theological-eschatological, ideas in terms of secularization. In my view, from the French Revolution onwards the great ideologies of the nineteenth and twentieth centuries can and must be read according to this political theological perspective. More precisely, the debate emerged around the relation between politics and the Judeo-Christian tradition – all too evident in the intense debate between Schmitt and Peterson on Eusebian political theology. It emerged from the confrontation between Eusebius of Caesarea – the ideologist of the Constantinian Age who supported a close relation of earthly and celestial monarchies – and Peterson who maintained that Christianity is not adaptable to this kind of monarchism, since the Christian God is not the simple One, but *Deus Trinitas*. The relation internal to this God makes Christianity unamenable to any form of political theology, of *religio civilis* – these are the terms of the polemic between Schmitt and Peterson. In my view, both positions are but two sides of the same coin since Western history can be characterized as a conflict, that is to say a conflict that unites, a *cum-fligere* between a political theological dimension that appeals, precisely, to a principle of authority and thus to the reduction of multiplicity to unity, and another that emphasizes mediation and exalts the moment of representation: you are not the absolute monarch, you are those who you represent: 'Representation' means to be in relation.

EP: *Is the latter the more problematic side of the coin?*

MC: Yes indeed, but above all because it is never distinguishable from the other side of the conflict. Thus my books such as *The*

Withholding Power, The Geo-philosophy of Europe, The Archipelago and others, as well as my research devoted to political philosophy insist on the thesis that while contradiction and conflict are European and European ailments, its *insanity* (*insania*), their cure can only be fatal, since their very life consists in this *insanity*, or *insecuritas*. It is necessary to sustain, to bear or literally *tolerate* this contradiction. This is what led me to explore this theme in terms of political theology, and more specifically in terms of a 'potere che frena' that you translate as 'withholding power'.

EP: *I'd like to ask about the title of the book –* Il potere che frena *– and the two senses that you seem to give it. From the outset you insist that* katechein, *more than the act of restraining or holding back, means to 'contain' or to 'include in itself'. In English, following Schmitt, the term* katechon *is understood almost exclusively in terms of restraining or imposing restrictions and limits. However, there is another term in English – 'withholding' – which, like the Greek* katechein, *can be understood in terms of both restraint and containment. Translating the title as* The Withholding Power *emphasizes your attempt in the book to show that the* katechon *does not only restrain but also contains within itself that which has to be restrained. It is this that inaugurates a new approach to political theology that takes a certain distance from Schmitt. Do you think this choice captures your understanding of the* katechon, *the specificity of your contribution to the debate?*

MC: The translation convinces me in that, as I say in the book, my interest in the *katechon* goes back a long way. Already in *Dell Inizio* (*On Beginning*) there is a section on the *katechon*. It also seems right in that it emphasizes the paradox, that contradiction again, that the power to restrain does not consist solely in restraining the enemy that comes to me from without. It is a more complex figure and your translation renders the idea – difficult to say in Italian – that a power that restrains must at the same time contain as much as restrain. Indeed, the only way truly to restrain something is to contain it. And this is certainly paradoxical because this power that restrains – restrains what? – the Adversary, the *Antikeimenos, anomie,* etc. – must also contain it within itself. Augustine's political theology is perfectly aware of this; political power, law, the restrain of *anomie,* the *nomos* restrains *anomie* but it also contains it within itself. Paul insists that the law will never overcome sin because law and sin reciprocally contain one another. Where there is law there is sin, and sin contains the law and recreates the sin. In short, the translation 'withholding' is fine. There is for sure a restraining element in the *katechon,* one that impedes and blocks but the only way to really impede or block something it is to hold it within, to embrace and to encompass/understand it; only then can we think to truly restrain it.

EP: *The initial thought was to render it as* The Restraining Power...

MC: The 'restraining power' doesn't work, it is too reductive. Withholding is fine, to hold there, to hold back, this is the idea of the *katechon.* In this book the ideas that we are talking about are developed with the intention of clarifying the mystery, the enigma of the *katechon,* the *katechon* of Paul, that Schmitt reintroduced into the twentieth century, and of which I speak in the book and which we shall return to.

EP: *One of the problems I frequently encountered translating the book was finding a language adequate to the concepts issuing from the tradition of political theology. The translation had in a sense to follow the book's reconstruction of the cultural context to which this language belongs. If I have understood correctly, you adopt the term* Evo, *which translates the Latin* aevum *and the Greek* aion *to signify a time for which messianic time, the irruption of the eternal in the here and now, in the* hic et nunc, *is an issue. For linear time, you use the words* secolo *and* epoca. *The real difficulty was above all with the term* Evo, *which at an early stage I tried to translate according to context as 'eternity', the 'eternal' or the 'everlasting', even as the 'time of eternity' or 'everlasting time', always aware that these were inadequate renditions. Can you further clarify these terms?*

MC: 'Age' (*Evo*) derives in fact from the same root, is basically the same term as *aion* but I am not really offering a translation of this term here. 'Age', in the sense I use it in the book, signifies the way, as Heidegger would say, in which 'being' is seen, interpreted, hearkened to in the course of an entire epoch. 'Age' indicates a period characterized by a determinate concept of being, not by this or that political or social fact. From this point of view 'Age' is meant in a sense similar to Hegel's when he speaks of the 'Romantic', he does not mean 'Romanticism' he means the way in which classical Greek and Roman culture pass over and are overcome by Christianity, that is what is meant by Age. Thus I distinguish 'Age' from epoch (*epoca*) because the idea of Age as opposed to epoch contains something of the eternal. *Aion* for Plato means exactly this, the confrontation between time (*chronos*) and the eternal. It did not originally refer to the eternal, but to life, a life that is full, complete – your *aion* is all your life, from beginning to end. This is the original meaning of the term; it became *aion* precisely because of the idea of completeness, of an accomplished form – and is adopted by philosophical language to mean the eternal, not in the sense of duration but of completion. It is for this reason that I imply or take Age to mean an accomplished epoch, emphasizing completion and not becoming. For all the reasons above, translating *Evo* as the 'timeless' will not do because it is a negative, privative term while 'eternal' and 'everlasting' give a sense of duration rather than completion, so it's better to translate *Evo* as 'Age', that is a completed epoch understood by analogy with the life of a person that has assumed its form, and this achieved form is in some sense eternal, abiding.

EP: *One of the main themes of your research is the concept of 'secularization' or the time or epoch in which human existence is reduced to an absolute immanence, to the point at which everything can be calculated and predicted in advance. But does 'secularization' really abolish every transcendence or does it conserve an idea of 'transcendence' given that humans, as you say, 'ek-sist' in so far as they can transcend themselves?*

MC: We are talking about a secularization that is not conscious of itself. In secularization the idea of self-transcendence appears as secularized for the secularized idea of self-transcendence is the idea of progress. What is the idea of progress if not the secularization of the idea of man as the power of self-transcendence? What is the difference? The traditional idea of transcendence has a vertical dimension, transcendence is not the movement from one point of the horizontal plane to another, nor is it the self-transcendence of continual progress, but it is the irruption of the eternal in the here and now (*hic et nunc*) that constitutes epochs and ages. This distinction is enormously significant and helps us understand that secularization indeed reduces human existence to an absolute immanence. And how did this secularization come about? Precisely, by aligning the dynamics of self-transcendence with the purely horizontal plane.

EP: *The net?*

MC: Yes, and hence my drawing the image of the net in the play between the symbol of the net and the symbol of the cross. It is a critique of secularization but in the Kantian sense of establishing the conditions of its possibility, not in the sense of taking it to be false or mistaken. It is the case that the idea of progress is today understood increasingly in purely quantitative terms. Once, in the ideology of the nineteenth century, the idea of progress was progress towards an end or goal, still immanent, but a goal nevertheless. This idea of a goal and this sense of progress gradually faded away and became increasingly indifferent. Progress is today becoming not only something situated on the horizontal plane, in the secular, but even without meaning insofar as it involves a process without end or goal, infinite in the sense of an infinite procedure. A transcendence that by now is completely secularized, a self-transcendence in the *saeculum*, in the sense of the secular.

EP: *One of the major terms in the edifice of the* katechon *for you is anomia. Contra Schmitt, who understands anomia as a species of anarchy, you see* anomie *(and not anarchy so much) as the main threat. In your thought,* anomie *is neither hostile to nor lacks organization; it is not some form of atheism and it does not seek to set up a new law. It has one single task: actively to destroy faith in Christ, faith in universal salvation. This destructive force is internally organized and ordered (the opposite of anarchy) and it seems to resemble the bureaucratic-administrative structures that organize our everyday life. Could you elaborate on the difference between your and Schmitt's understanding of* anomie?

MC: There is a significant difference. Schmitt tends to see the *anomos*, i.e., the coming or unfolding of the Antichrist, whom Schmitt tracks down to the beginning of the French Revolution, as the dissolution of the *nomos* of the earth, the dissolution of the European states; he looks upon all this without any reactionary nostalgia. Although Schmitt is not an old-fashioned philosopher of the Restoration, in the sense that he sought to promote the restoration of the *ancien régime*, nonetheless he understands the *anomos* in terms of anarchy, but that is not all. He always understands the bearers, the protagonists of this anarchy to be the people. This is the most disturbing element of his thought and one that brings him closer to the thought of Donoso Cortés and De Maistre, and to all the grand Restoration philosophies. Anarchy (*anomie* in Schmitt) has always mustered its popular troops (*milites*), its energies and forces; *anomie* is always born from below and storms the castle of the élite. The fate of this spirit that wells up from below and is guided by the *anomos* – the impersonal *anomos* – is doomed to overcome any élite, any aristocracy and any *katechon*. This view of Schmitt shows his proximity to the philosophy of Restoration, although he never dreamt of saying that the *ancien régime* could ever oppose *anomie*. That was his great blunder. The *ancien régime* had no part in the conservative revolution, and the conservative revolution was perfectly aware it had no weapons against *anomie*; perhaps, Schmitt muses, Hitler had them, but he too came from the people. Schmitt thought that the possibility of a real *katechon* might lie with the people, a *katechon* that will oppose the very same anomic energies that originate in the people. This was his great error. If power is only the power of an élite, of an aristocracy that can still possess catechontic energy then it would be no more, since *anomie* has already destroyed it or is still destroying it. This is basically Schmitt's pessimistic vision. In order to place it in its historical context, it is necessary to take into account the relationship his thought has to some aspects of the conservative revolution but also to Spengler, to Jünger and, in short, all the Pre-Nazi German milieu that partly compromised with Nazism, but the majority of whom like Ernest Jünger, his brother, and Gottfried Benn retreated into an internal exile. The internal exile of those who remained in Germany but had no alternative to speak of, who mounted no opposition and who, unlike Schmitt or Heidegger, were certainly not involved with Nazism. And this is the problem with Schmitt, against whom my polemic is aimed, the *anomos* does not appear as anarchy, it is not anarchy. I must insist on this difference; *anomos* is not anarchy, nor is it anarchy in the thought of Paul or in John's *Book of Revelation*, nor is it parsed like anarchy. It is a weak interpretation that does not do justice to the real problem which is to interpret *anomie* as a *Gestell*, a system. Here my view is closer to Heidegger's, or Severino's in Italy, than to Schmitt's.

EP: *Indeed,* anomie *is an organized system.*

MC: Yes, it appears as such, if not it could not be a *katechon*, the figure of the *katechon* would make no sense. The *katechon* does not primarily oppose the mere unfolding of evil but the one who wants to be worshipped, and to be worshipped as God. However, worship means *religio*: organization, and *religio civilis* means the ordering of worship, as the Romans came to recognize well. There is no worship without organization, without ordering. Anarchy is not a worship, it does not have a cult. For this reason the spirit of anarchy has nothing to do with the *anomos* or with *anomie*. This is where the greatest misunderstanding originates, the misunderstanding of all conservative revolutions, and of Jünger even. In his *On the Marble Cliffs*, for example, the *anomos* is clearly understood as anarchy but that cannot be so.

EP: *You frequently insist that* anomos *is the one who rejects the law of the Gospel.*

MC: Yes, *anomos* is not the one who rejects the law *tout court* but the law of the Gospel, the law of 'glad tidings'. Schmitt commits a philological error in the interpretation of the play between the *katechon* and *anomie*.

EP: *Your book examines various candidates for the* katechon: *Empire, Church and the Grand Inquisitor. The first two preserve, through the aporetic and contradictory discharge of catechontic functions, the commerce between transcendence and immanence. The third, though, stands for a different kind of difficulty. The Grand Inquisitor, 'one of us', a dignitary of the Church devoted to the language, ideas and practices of the eschatological horizon, views Christ himself and the freedom he represents as the great threat. For a* katechon *in the form of the Grand Inquisitor, it is Christ who should be the 'target' of catechontic restraint. Do you think that in our age all catechontic function is like the Grand Inquisitor, that is to say, at the service of* anomie?

MC: The *katechon* is a complex figure and so is the figure of the Antichrist. The Antichrist too contains many elements and persons, and the Christian tradition clearly spells that out. When Augustine asked himself 'could it be that I am the Antichrist?' he meant to say that the Antichrist sometimes could take on the appearance of Augustine. That is, they are complex figures. They are like the figures of Giuseppe Arcimboldo that are composed of many faces, of many masques, never *simplex et unum*, with none of these figures being more prominent than the other. For that reason these figures are of great political significance. In politics there is nothing of the geometric-mathematic simplicity of Spinoza's ethics. And Spinoza is very well aware of that in his *Tractatus Theologico-Politicus*. Politics is a passionate field, a field where passion and reason entwine and that is the case for the *katechon*, for the *anomos* and for all those figures that one encounters in the theological political register. Thus there are a variety of candidates and there's no dominant candidate. The *katechon* is necessarily a complex figure because he/it must face the *anomos*. *Anomie* is an equally complex figure that, unlike confused anarchy, has its own dimensions, cultural, political dimensions; it does not only clearly contrast with the *katechon* and catechontic powers but it also contrasts with worshipping the true God; it has as many dimensions as the Antichrist, commercial and economic ones but also a religious dimension, as is written in the *Book of Revelation*. It is therefore a *Gestell*, a system. Moreover, the *katechon* must necessarily resemble *anomie* to the degree it restrains and contains it. In the book I try to convey the idea of such complexity unlike the way it sometimes appears in Schmitt and in the debates following his contributions. Clearly, the most disturbing figure, at least the figure that disturbs me the most, is the Grand Inquisitor. That empire has a catechontic function can in a certain way be intuitively understood, and this is how it was understood by the majority of interpretations in the Christian tradition for whom empire was political power *par excellence* because it evidently opposed *anomie*. More difficult to understand is the Church. The Church holds the form of the Age in expectation of the *parousia*, yet if the *withholding* function were to be true, it must also contain ... and how can the Church contain the Antichrist, provided that in order to restrain it must also contain? The issue of attributing a catechontic function to the Church is already highly problematic but the interpreters of the Christian tradition, quoted in the book, have done so. Because the Church has an interest in maintaining the form of the Age while waiting for the *parousia*, this expectant waiting implies restraint, implies containing ... waiting for what? Waiting for the conversion of the people, the 'stubborn people' Israel?

EP: *It is because the Church structurally contains the Antichrist that its catechontic function is so problematic?*

MC: Precisely; while attributing catechontic functions to empire is fairly uncomplicated it is much more complex with regard to the Church. It becomes more complex still when we consider the Grand Inquisitor who grounds the necessity of his catechontic function, planning to resist at all costs, on a thoroughly Antichristic perspective. This is why the figure of the Grand Inquisitor is so disturbing. For his catechontic function, clearly one that opposes evil, pretends it will last for all eternity, as if it could, grounded as it is on an explicitly Antichristic import; that is to say, 'no, you, Christ, must not return, it were better you had never come, never existed, because you seduce, you deceive'. The role of seduction traditionally attributed to the Antichrist is attributed by the Grand Inquisitor himself to Christ. Christ is charged with deceiving men with the idea that they could be free. The Grand Inquisitor attacks head on the central message of the Gospel, which is that 'you are free'; for the basic meaning of the Gospel, which is that of our being the children of God made in His likeness and in His image, should be translated as 'you are as free as the Heavenly Father'. The Grand Inquisitor says, if there is to be a catechontic function, if we are to restrain evil that spills out from all sides but mainly from below (the demand for bread) then we must renounce Christ, renounce his role. The Antichrist does not deny the existence of Christ, let alone the existence of God, he denies the Messianic role, the redemptive character of Christ. It is the first appearance of a catechontic figure whose catechontic function is based on radically opposing the message of the Gospel; one who is *katechon* only to the degree that he completely contains within himself the Antichrist. A tragic figure who having encountered Christ in his life experienced the encounter as a ruin. He is a figure of the end of Christianity. It is in fact remarkable that it is Dostoyevsky who represents the encounter in this manner, Dostoyevsky the believer *par excellence* among the great European literatures and cultures of the past two centuries. Moreover, it is not clear who in the *Brothers Karamazov*, or elsewhere in Dostoyevsky, can really oppose the Grand Inquisitor; where is the logico-philosophical opposition, there is none. There is the act of Dostoyevsky, the believer who believes in what? In the impossible. The believer is one who thinks the impossible is possible. The Grand Inquisitor's declaration is logical, philosophical, rigorous whereas the believer thinks the impossible to be possible. What is this impossible-possible belief? That the human is free. This is what faith is.

EP: *In its troubled confrontation with secularization, can the Church still play a role today?*

MC: The Church is going through times of considerable internal reform but the most striking feature of our times is the decline of

Europe. Christianity, and if one cares to look will one see it in the gestures and actions of the present Pope, is geared to the disenchanted acknowledgement of the decline of the Christian world, and not so much in its adopted homelands as in Europe itself. The eye of the Church is now cast elsewhere, the task of carrying the message of the Gospel has migrated elsewhere, and this is a prodigious sign. It is a sign of our times, since the last Popes Wojtyla, Ratzinger, were still European Popes who lived through European dramas. At present, the vision of the current Pope and his Church strikes one as odd with regard to the problems we have been discussing, but I do not know … everything can admit of a double reading; from a certain point of view, all this can be understood as the overcoming of Eurocentrism, as a true global evangelizing mission, but on the other hand how can you not see it as a sign of disenchanted decline, as recognition of the twilight of Europe? Undoubtedly, Europe has been the sacred centre of Christendom; however, it is likewise clear that this Pope's focus has shifted from it, Europe is no longer the centre of the great cultural, social, ethical, political problems even those of this very continent, of the West in general. No longer the centre. Of that there is no doubt.

EP: *What of the Franciscan message of the present Pope?*

MC: The Franciscan message, a message of great reform, of poverty, is remarkable indeed. At the same time though, how can we forget that this is the first ever Jesuit Pope? It is an astonishing paradox that the first Jesuit Pope has taken the name of Francis. How can we not think that behind this arrangement there is a compromise typical of the Jesuit order? Compromise in the noblest, strongest, most momentous sense of the term? How can we not think of these things? Of the arrangement that allows one to keep everything as one must? Here too [with this Pope], we see the figure of the *katechon* that must retain and hold everything because contradictions ought not erupt; for that reason St Francis and Ignatius of Loyola are put together. Is the encounter between St Francis and Ignatius an eschatological sign or a historical compromise? How to tell? The message is Janus-faced and ambiguous and so is our state of being, in my view; this ambiguity can be fruitful and productive, while still ambiguous. The message of St Francis is not simply a message of charity and poverty: Francis was not so good nor so merciful; he had his own Christian doctrine that bordered on heresy, his own ideas about the relationship with the institutions of the Church and even his relationship with his own order. Francis did not only go about dispensing benedictions, it is certain that had he arrived in Assisi and seen an enormous church being built to contain his simple Porziuncula chapel he would have taken a hammer to it. To repeat, the Pope's message is an eschatological sign, it is viewed as the eschatological sign of a new Church that somehow extraordinarily unifies all these traditions. What is the ground of this unification? A new doctrine of poverty, of mercy or a Jesuitical compromise in the noblest and most momentous sense of the term? We have to think on these matters because the Church cannot renounce its catechontic function. The structural contradiction of the Church is that it is a political form and as such it will be with us until the end.

EP: *The Italian Catholic Church in particular?*

MC: But there are no national religions anymore, there is only Catholicism and the rest is *saeculum* and that is that. American religion, for example, is a *religio civilis*, empires must have a religion and the American one is a mixture, an American *religio*, as Bloom calls it. Great states cannot exist without a cultural religious dimension, so the USA have made a *religio civilis* out of a Christian pastiche. The problem is the Catholic Church and in part the Orthodox Church too, now that Russia has been reborn into the shape of an empire, Orthodoxy being an essential and structural element of Russian politics, and for that reason the discourse of political theology still holds there. Orthodoxy: it is true that there is a competition with it that no Pope has managed to overcome, even when there's good will on both sides, as with the Patriarch of Constantinople, Bartholomew. So we should not speak of Orthodoxy *tout court* but of Russian Orthodoxy, of the Russian Autochephalous Church, the great Russian Church with its great tradition, its problems of a theological character, all these are big issues. There is a problem for political theology in the United States too, for empires must have a cult. To understand empires, you also have to contend with their – let's call them – 'theologies' and this is definitely not the case for any European country, any European regime.

EP: *Given the situation in Europe, as you have described it, what of the Italian political theology debate?*

MC: In Italy unlike elsewhere the political theology debate has been broader and richer. The relationship between theology and philosophy is a theme much more mined here than elsewhere. For sure, in France there has been the work of Paul Ricoeur, particularly in the field of Judaic thought and its relation to political philosophy. In Italy the works of Vincenzo Vitiello, Piero Coda, Bruno Forte and many others devote much attention to this particular theme. However while the works of Giacomo Marramao, Roberto Esposito, Giorgio Agamben that expound on themes of political philosophy by emphasizing the theological aspect have been of particular interest, I don't think that in the European cultural panorama political philosophy addresses the theological aspect in the way it does in Italy. An important aspect of this strand of Italian political philosophy, fairly known outside Italy, is to be found in Gramsci, arguably one of the better known Italian thinkers abroad. In his thoughts on hegemony and elsewhere, he devotes much attention to elements of religion. His brand of Marxism is interested in those elements that the old Marxists would have treated as mere superstructure. For Gramsci both political philosophy and political science have to achieve relevance by their own means and not be materialistically reduced to the relation between politics and social structure, class structure and economic relations or relations of production. Far from this classical Marxist view Gramsci paid attention to all these aspects, the ideological, the philosophical, the religious. All these are central to Gramsci. So there's all this attention to theological political aspects in the tradition hailing from Gramsci and from Italian Marxism that one does not find in the liberal tradition, in Croce for example. Croce was truly deaf to these problems, unlike the Marxists. So the origin is Gramsci, the way the problem of hegemony is posed in his thought, and in a certain sense Giovanni Gentile too, since his *Genesis and Structure of Society* is very Gramscian, or maybe Gramsci is very Gentilian. In fact many, if not all, of Gentile's followers became communists in the post-war years. Augusto Del Noce has, in my view, written some very interesting things on the link between Gramscianism and Actualism. And Gentile's *Genesis and Structure of Society* is a wonderful book. He deserves to be more widely known.

EP: *You often return to the idea of decline, of twilight, a famous Nietzschean theme; how can this twilight be lived?*

MC: We are now living through the collapse of the West as the dominant power, as empire. I don't mean the collapse of European empires since those collapsed at the end of World War One. We are living through a long twilight, whether it can have any golden hues nobody knows. We did not and cannot decide on this twilight but we may decide how to act and be placed in it. By resisting? By opposing it, by desperately trying to endure it? Hegel argued that the greatness of a civilization can only be seen in its twilight, only when it has come to an end can we say whether it was beautiful or not. That is one way of living in the twilight. But if you instead cling to the remnants of power, your revenues, then you will embarrass yourself. The European twilight should take sustenance from its load-bearing ideas, from its great saints from St Francis onwards, the themes of equality, of hospitality, etc., don't you agree? This is how our wane should be. That is, set down the will to power for if you remain pitifully attached to its miserable remnants then your twilight will stink. I think this is how we have chosen to live our twilight, by clinging to such miserable remnants of power.

EP: *In the last chapter of the book you speak of the 'apparatus' that incrementally confirms and reinforces the West's will to power, but this will bring the apparatus, now at the far end of its decline, before the mouth of the abyss. Can we say that you are in search of the 'hidden' in Christian theology, in a way similar to Heidegger's, who thought of Western metaphysics in terms of concealment and unconcealment? Heidegger too often speaks of Ge-stell, of apparatus.*

MC: On this the philosopher remains silent; as you know, the owl of Minerva flies only at dusk. What is certain is that we are in a time of crisis for all catechontic powers, of the Church in its time of transition, I don't see on the horizon figures like the Grand Inquisitor, even though many act like him maintaining that Christianity is finished, that Christ failed; they don't say it explicitly but they act like it. There are no genuine empires, that is the present state of affairs. A state, as I say in the last chapter, of great crises, of the destruction of all traditional catechontic powers; what is going to succeed them? One can neither know nor say. Clearly the last twenty years have disenchanted any idea that future catechontic powers can be like the two victorious titans emerging after the last war, can be like those that shaped the world in the 50 years following World War Two. The two great catechontic forces, whose conflict kept the world in balance for 40–50 years, the USA and the USSR, are not now capable in any way to continue doing so. The USA delude themselves that after the collapse of the USSR they are the only empire, a democratic empire, empire in the sense of *auctoritas* that shows the way, maps a direction. In that they have tragically failed, piling disaster on disaster in chasing this utopia. I cannot think of any so-called imperial power that has as many disasters to its name as the USA in the last twenty years, randomly destabilizing the world, without any prospect, without any idea of what should come after, simply on the basis of ideology, utopias, of very short-term interests. Perhaps the USA, had they been well guided, could have become a worldly *auctoritas* but now they too have caved in. And what may the new catechontic powers be? How am I to know, perhaps China? By what means and through what future paths? *Hic sunt leones.*

EP: *The very last line of your book reads like this, 'Prometheus has withdrawn ... Epimetheus is at large and in our world opening ever newer Pandora's boxes'. How are we to understand Hope, the last gift left in Pandora's box? As a poisoned gift, a pure illusion or a thrownness in the sense of being open to a future?*

MC: Hope is an ambiguous term, on the one hand there is hope that can be the ultimate evil because it blinds and on the other there is hope that can be hope, that lives in your awareness of this disenchanted twilight and shows you how to be rid of your will to power; such is good hope. Being rid of the will to power must be shown, must be embodied as in St Francis who did not preach sermons but embodied his poverty and so the meaning of his poverty. Like him, you could embody and signify some elements of your culture or your civilization that are not connected to the will to power, or better still that manifest the overthrowing of the will to power. Are there any such elements in our culture? For sure, you see them in Schopenhauer, in Nietzsche, Heidegger, even in science, when it is not merely linked to technology and the latter's will to power but when it is viewed as contemplation of nature. And this despite Emanuele Severino's conviction that the latter is not possible, that it is a utopia, absolute enchantment. When scientists hunt down origins, are they not serving speculative ends? I don't think such research can have immediate technological application. For certain, to build a 500 million kilometre accelerator is business but an absurd and paradoxical business, a single great machine to enable us to see the origin of the universe. Supposedly we come to see it at some point and then what? That would be all, as when we saw the moon?

EP: *Science is a wonderment?*

MC: Yes, wonderment is an essential element of science. *Thaumazein*, why not value it?

Bibliography

Alighieri, Dante (1903) *The Banquet*, transl. Philip H. Wickstool, John Dent and Co., London.

Alighieri, Dante (2003) *Monarchy*, transl. Prue Shaw, Cambridge University Press, Cambridge.

Alighieri, Dante (2012) *The Divine Comedy*, transl. Robin Kirkpatrick, Penguin Classics, London.

Alzati, C. (ed.) *Impero: un concetto dimenticato del diritto publico in christinita*.

Aristotle (1987) The Ethics of Aristotle, *The Nicomachean Ethics*, transl. J.A.K. Thomson, Penguin Books, London.

Augustine (2003) *City of God*, transl. Henry Bettenson, Penguin Books, Harmondsworth.

Barth, Karl (1968) *The Epistles to Romans*, transl. Edwyn C. Hoskyns, Oxford University Press, Oxford.

Bettiolo, Paolo and Filoramo, Giovanni (eds) (2002) *Il dio mortale. Teologie politiche tra. antico e contemporaneo*, Morcelliana Brescia.

Bultmann, Rudolf Karl (1971) *The Gospel of John: A Commentary*, Westminster John Knox Press, Louisville.

Cacciari, Massimo and Esposito, Roberto (2014) 'Dialogo sulla teleologia politica', *Micromega* 2/2014.

Catalano, Pierangelo (1983) Alcuni sviluppi del concetto giuridico di '*imperium populi Romani*', in *Popoli e spazio romano tra diritto e profezia*, Edizioni Scientifiche Italiana, Napoli.

Catalano, Pierangelo (2000) Impero: un concetto dimenticato del diritto publico, in *Cristianità ed Europa. Miscellanea di studi in onore di Luigi Prosdocimi*, ed. Cesare Alzati, Roma-Freiburg-Wien.

Caygill, Howard (2011) 'Historiography and Political Theology:
    Momigliano and the End of History', Alexandra Lianieri (ed.),
    The Western Time of Ancient History: Historiographical Encounters
    with Greek and Roman Pasts, Cambridge University Press,
    Cambridge.

Coldagelli, Umberto (2005) *Vita di Tocqueville*, Donzelli, Roma.

Descartes, René (1985) *Cogitationes Privatae* in *The Philosophical Writings
    of Descartes, Vol. I*, transl. John Cottingham, Robert Stoothoff and
    Dugald Murdoch, Cambridge University Press, Cambridge.

Donoso Cortés, Juan (2000) Letter to Cardinal Fornari on the Errors of Our
    Times in *Selected Works of Juan Donoso Cortés*, transl. Jeffrey P. Johnson,
    Greenwood Press, Westport.

Duso, Giuseppe (2003) *La rappresentanza politica: genesi e crisi del
    concetto*, FrancoAngeli, Milano.

Gaeta, Giancarlo (2002) Teologia e politica in Paolo a proposito
    dell'esegesi dei Romani 13 in *Il dio Mortale*, cit.

Galli, G. (2012) Le teologie politiche di Carl Schmitt, in *Democrazie e
    religioni. La sfida degli incompatibili?*, eds Mario Ruggenini, Roberta
    Dreon and Sebastiano Galanti Grollo, Donzelli Roma.

Givone, Sergio (1984) *Dostoevskij e la filosofia*, Laterza, Roma-Bari.

Grossheutschi, Felix (1996) *Carl Schmitt und die Lehre vom Katechon*,
    Duncker & Humblot, Berlin.

Hobbes, Thomas (1651; 1991) *Leviathan (The Matter Form and Power of a
    Commowealth Ecclesiastical and Civil*, Cambridge University Press,
    Cambridge.

Hofmann, Hasso (1974) *Repräsentation. Studien zur Wort- und
    Begriffsgeschichte von der Antike bis ins 19. Jahrhundert*, Duncker &
    Humblot, Berlin.

Idel, Mosche (1998) *Messianic Mystics*, Yale University Press, New Haven,
    London.

Irti, Natalino (2006) *Norma e luoghi. Problemi di geo-diritto*, Laterza,
    Roma-Bari.

Jünger, Ernst (1930; 1993) *Total Mobilisation, The Heidegger Controversy,
    A Critical Reader*, ed. Richard Wolin. The MIT Press, Cambridge, MA
    and London, pp. 122–139.

Jünger, Ernst (1932; 2007) *Der Arbeiter. Herrschaft und Gestalt.* Klett-Cotta,
    Stuttgart.

Jünger, Ernst (1934; 1942) *Blätter und Steine*, Hamburg Hanseatische Verlagstat, Hamburg.

Jünger, Ernst (1939; 1970) *On the Marble Cliffs*, transl. Stuart Hood, Penguin Books, London.

Jünger, Ernst (1953) *Der gordischen Knoten*, Klostermann, Frankfurt.

Jünger, Ernst (1959; 2013) *An der Zeitmauer*, Klett-Cotta, Stuttgart.

Jünger, Ernst (1960) *Der Weltstaat: Organismus und Organisation*, Ernst Klett, Stuttgart.

Jünger, Ernst (1987) *Zwei Mal Halley*, Klett-Cotta, Stuttgart.

Kojève, Alexandre (1941; 2014) *The Notion of Authority*, transl. Hager Veslati, Verso, New York, London.

Kojève, Alexandre and Schmitt, Carl (2001) *The Correspondence*, transl. Erik De Vries, in *Interpretation*, 29/1, pp. 91–130.

Lambertini, Roberto (2009) Un'esegesi 'militante' di 2 Ts, 2 all'Università di Parigi nel XIII secolo. Il 'Tractatus de Antichristo et eius ministris', in *Il 'Katéchon' (2 Ts, 2, 6–7) e L'Anticristo*, op. cit.

Lettieri, Gaetano (2002) *Riflessioni sulla teologia poltica in Agostino*, in *Il dio mortale*, cit.

Macchiavelli, Niccolò (1994), *The Prince*, transl. Russell Price and Quentin Skinner, Cambridge University Press, Cambridge.

De Maistre, Joseph Marie (1850) *The Pope, Considered in his Relations to the Chuch, Temporal Sovereignities, Separated Churches and the Cause of Civilisation*, transl. Aeneas Dawson, London.

Maraviglia, Massimo (2006) *La penultima guerra. Il katékon nella dottrina dell'ordine politico di Carl Schmitt*, LED Edizioni Universitarie, Milan.

Marramao, Giacomo (2009) *Passagio a Occidente. Filosofia e globalizzazione*, Bollati Boringhieri, Turin.

Marramao, Giacomo (2013) *Dopo il Leviatano. Individuo e communità*, Bollati Boringhieri, Turin.

Mazzarino, Santo (2010) *L'Impero Romano*, Laterza, Bari-Roma.

Metzger, Paul (2008/2009) Il 'Katéchon'. Una fondazione esegetica, in *Il 'Katéchon' (2 Ts, 2, 6–7) e l'Anticristo. Teologia e politica di fronte al mistero dell'anomia*, Politica e Religione 2008/2009, Morcelliana-Brescia.

Momigliano, Arnaldo (1987) *Storia e storiagrafia antica*, Il Mulino, Bologna.

Münkler, Herfried (2007) *Empires: The Logic of World Domination from Ancient Rome to the United States,* transl. Patrick Camiller, Polity, Malden, MA.

Musil, Robert (1997) *The Man Without Qualities,* transl. Sophie Wilkins and Burton Pike, Picador, London.

Nardi, Bruno (1967) *Saggi di filosofia dantesca,* La Nuova Italia, Firenze.

Nicoletti, Michele (1990) *Trascendenza e Potere. La teologia politica di Carl Schmitt,* Morcelliana, Brescia.

Nicoletti, Michele (ed.) (2008–2009) *Il 'Katéchon' (2 Ts, 2: 6–7) e l'Anticristo. Teologia e politica di fronte al mistero dell'anomia,* in *Politica e Religione, Politica e religion,* Morcelliana, Brescia.

Panattoni, Riccardo (2001) *Appartenenza e eschaton: la lettera ai Romani di san Paolo e la questione teologico politica,* Liguori, Napoli.

Pareyson, Luigi (1993) *Dostoyevkij: Filosofia, romanzo ed esperienza religiosa,* Einaudi, Torino.

Pesce, Mauro (1986) Marginalità e sottomissione, la concezione escatologica del potere in Paolo in *Cristianesimo e potere,* eds Paolo Prodi and L. Sartori, EDB, Bologna.

Peterson, Erik (1933) *Die Kirche aus Juden und Heiden.* Drei Vorlesungen, Pustet, Salzburg.

Peterson, Erik (1935; 2011) Monotheism as a Political Problem, in *Theological Tractates (Cultural Memory in the Present),* transl. Michael J. Hollerich, Stanford University Press, Stanford.

Pitta, A (2001) *Lettere ai romani,* San Paolo, Milano.

Potestà, Gianluca and Rizzi, Marco (eds) (2005) *L'Anticristo,* Fondazione Lorenzo Valla, A. Mondadori, Rome-Milan.

Ratzinger, Joseph (2008) *Church, Ecumenism and Politics: New Endeavours in Ecclesiology,* Ignatius Press, Rome.

Rauchensteiner, Meinhard and Seitter, Walter (eds) (2001) Nr. 25, Katechonten, Den Untergang aufhalten, Syndikat/Philo, Berlin.

Rigaux, Bèda (1959) *Saint Paul: Les Épîtres aux Thessaloniciens,* Gabalda, Paris.

Rizzi, Marco (2008/2009) Storia di un inganno (ermeneutico): il 'Katéchon' e il Anticristo nelle interpretazioni del II e III secolo della 'Seconda lettera ai Tessalonicesi' in *Il 'Katéchon' (2 Ts, 2, 6–7) e l'Anticristo, cit.* Morcelliana, Brescia.

Rozanov, Vasily (1977) *The Apocalypse of Our Time and Other Writings,* transl. Robert Payne, Praeger Publishers, New York.

Schmitt, Carl (1950) *Donoso Cortes in gesamteuropäischer Interpretation,* Duncker & Humblot, Berlin.

Schmitt, Carl (1950) *Ex captivitate salus. Erinnerungen der Zeit 1945/47*, Greven Verlag, Köln.

Schmitt, Carl (1985) *Political Theology: Four Chapters on the Concept of Sovereignty*, transl. George D. Schwab, MIT Press, Chicago, MA.

Schmitt, Carl (1991) *Glossarium. Aufzeichnungen der Jahre 1947–1951*, ed. Eberhard Freiherr von Medem, Duncker & Humblot, Berlin.

Schmitt, Carl (2006) *The Nomos of the Earth in the International Law of Jus Publicum Europeum*, transl. G.L. Ulmen, Telos Press Publishing, New York.

Schmitt, Carl (2009) *Three Possibilities for a Christian Conception of History,* transl. Mario Wenning, Telos 147, Summer 2009, pp. 167–170.

Schmitt, Carl (2015) *Dialogues on Power and Space*, transl. Samuel Garrett Zeitlin, Polity Press, Cambridge, UK.

Scholem, Gershom Gerhard (1959; 1994) Toward an Understanding of the Messianic Idea in Judaism, in *The Messianic Idea in Judaism*, transl. Michael A. Meyer, Schocken, New York.

Siniscalco, Paolo (2007) *Il cammino di Cristo nell'Impero romano*, Laterza, Bari-Roma.

Spinoza, Benedict de (1996) *Ethics*, transl. Edwin Curley, Penguin Classics, London.

Taubes, Jacob (2003) *En divergent accord: à propos de Carl Schmitt*, Payot & Rivages, Paris.

Taubes, Jacob (2003) *Political Theology of Paul*, transl. Dana Hollander, Stanford University Press, Stanford.

Taylor, Charles (2007) *A Secular Age*, Harvard University Press, Cambridge, MA.

Virgil (2003) *Aeneid*, transl. David West, Penguin Classics, London.

Virgil (2009) *Georgics*, transl. Peter Fallon and Elaine Fantham, Oxford World's Classics, Oxford.

Weber, Max (1922; 1978) *Economy and Society*, eds Gunther Roth and Claus Wittich, University of California Press, Berkeley.

Weber, Max (2004) Politics as a Vocation, in *The Vocation Lectures*, transl. Rodney Livingstone, Hackett Publishing Company, Indianapolis/ Cambridge.

Index